# JOURNEY

## *of a*

# LAKOTA ELDER

*A memoir written to inspire women of color*

## WYNNE DUBRAY

iUniverse, Inc.
Bloomington

Journey of a Lakota Elder
A memoir written to inspire women of color

iUniverse books may be ordered through booksellers or by contacting:

iUniverse
1663 Liberty Drive
Bloomington, IN 47403
www.iuniverse.com
1-800-Authors (1-800-288-4677)

ISBN: 978-1-4759-6210-9 (sc)
ISBN: 978-1-4759-6211-6 (ebk)

Library of Congress Control Number: 2012921569

Printed in the United States of America

iUniverse rev. date: 11/21/2012

# *Dedication*

This book is dedicated to my children, David, Diane, Les, Gary, Peter, and Joseph.

# Table of Contents

# *Acknowledgement*

I wish to acknowledge those who spearheaded my career and gave me endless support and encouragement: Dr. Pat Purcelle, Ron Boltz, Dr. Bea Medicine, Judson Albertson, and Joseph Lipoma. I also thank Dr. Adelle Sanders for editing the transcript for the memoirs. Finally, I offer a special thanks to the thousands of students who enhanced my teaching career by challenging my thinking over the years and the thousands of clients in therapy who shared with me the strength of the human spirit.

# *Foreword*

In order to break the bonds of colonization and heal our historical trauma, we, as Native people, must debunk stories told about us and the histories written about us by those who did not walk our paths or journey. We need to decolonize ourselves. To do this we need to write our own histories. In light of this decolonization movement occurring in Indian country, Dr. DuBray has penned her journey. She was written her memoirs to share her history.

Throughout the following pages, the reader gets a glimpse of Dr. DuBray's journey and her world view. She also delineates her publications and her leadership role in the social work field, as well as her contribution to mentoring students of social work. Through your journey through this book, it is hoped you will get a feel for Dr. DuBray's path in life and her lasting contribution she made.

Adelle Sanders

# Introduction

It was a cold spring morning when I made my debut on the harsh and lonely prairie of South Dakota on April 22, 1932. As my father held me in his arms he named me Winona for being a very old spirit and Fern for the protection I would need as a physically fragile child. I had asthma during most of my childhood and required special care and attention from my parents and siblings.

I was born the ninth of ten children to a poor Lakota couple in a log cabin built by the hands and sweat of my father. The location was on the extended Rosebud Lakota reservation in South Dakota. I believe I had been here before but failed to learn the great lessons of life that would free me from future visits.

So on this cold brisk morning, Winona Fern DuBray met her parents for the first time. I do not know why I chose these parents except for the expectation that they would teach me how to transcend the limitations of mortality, if only in my imagination.

I had a vague memory of a past life roaming the prairie as a great Lakota chief only to be forced into submission by an unfriendly group of Wasi'chus hell bent on destroying everything they touched. The earth remembers that sadness that still hovers over the prairie and the once Great Lakota Nation. This was after the Lakota were led into captivity. Their freedom vanished in one generation to be replaced by the wardship held over them by the federal government.

I did not know how, when, or why but this Lakota would some day be transplanted in a land far away. My love for learning would not be satisfied here on the prairie but opportunities would be available in another place in another time. I could see a vision of that life on a daily basis.

I have always been an achiever. My standard of excellence came from within, and was not externally imposed. As a perfectionist and an achiever it was no surprise that I would end up in academia. The challenge of academia was attractive primarily because the parameters and the depth of knowledge could never be mastered.

The Lakota culture was my launching pad. The Lakota culture is steeped in symbolism, metaphor, and abstract thinking. With a strong sense of history the Lakota, like other oppressed people, are always reminded of the grave injustices imposed on our people. As spiritual people we have always been aware of the dangers of greed and materialism and the impact of these on humanity. Unfortunately, the scars of oppression have robbed many Lakota from the ability to achieve their true potential.

This memoir must begin with a historical overview of my ancestors in order for the reader to grasp the meaning and the content of the following pages. Therefore, I begin with a sketch of life on the plains to allow the reader to visualize how and when my story all began.

# *Chapter 1*

# Historical Overview of the Lakota Tribe

The Lakota, referred to as Sioux, were first encountered by white explorers about 1640 in the Woodland region just west of the Great Lakes. Lakota territory consisted of what is now the southern two-thirds of the state of Minnesota. The tribe subsisted on hunting and fishing and the gathering of wild plant foods, as well as some horticulture.

The Lakota were forced to move westward onto the plains. By 1750, they had begun to cross the Missouri River and filter into the Black Hills region. The tribe consisted of three divisions, the Nakota, Dakota, and Lakota. By 1800, horses were becoming plentiful on the Northern Plains, and the horse facilitated the hunting of buffalo. The Lakota abandoned their horticulture and came to depend primarily on the buffalo for food.

Until the 1840s the only white men the Lakota had known were the traders and trappers who lived very much like themselves. Hostilities between the Lakota and the whites increased, as the settlers looked with greedy eyes on the vast plains controlled by the Lakota.

In 1868, gold was discovered in the Black Hills, and a gold rush was underway. The Black Hills are a sacred place to the Lakota and, at that time, were part of the vast Lakota reservation which included most of South Dakota and parts of North Dakota, Wyoming, Montana, and Nebraska. The U.S. Army seized control of the Black Hills in direct violation of the existing treaty, and the last Lakota War commenced. General George Armstrong Custer learned how well the Lakota could fight. Custer, through his own arrogance and stupidity, led his men to certain death at the battle of the Little Big Horn on June 5, 1876.

He was no match for such fighting men as Crazy Horse, Gall, and Sitting Bull. It was a great victory, but by 1877, most of the Lakota were back on their reservation, then considerably reduced in size. The U.S. government has never forgotten this humiliating defeat and has punished the Lakota ever since.

On August 15, 1876, Congress, fired up by Custer's defeat decided it would no longer bargain with the Lakota. Congress passed the Sioux Appropriation Bill, which was a demand for unconditional surrender. The Lakota would receive no more rations or help of any kind until they gave up the Black Hills and everything west of the Black Hills. Only ten percent of the Lakota signed this agreement. This agreement violated the Treaty of 1868 which required that three fourths of the adult males in the tribe would have to sign any document before it would go into effect. On February 18, 1877, Congress passed the Act of 1877, which declared that the U.S. government had the right to take the property of the Lakota nation away from the tribe.

In 1899, another treaty was forced upon the Lakota which took half of what lands still remained. Simultaneously, appropriations for the Native American reservations were cut by Congress; this was monies that had been promised to the tribes in return for giving up their lands. Now that the Lakota were no longer considered a military threat, Congress felt secure enough to reduce the funds intended for feeding and caring for the tribe. Disease and starvation swept across the reservations. Thousands of Lakota people perished from malnutrition and tuberculosis. In fact, my maternal grandparents perished.

The Act of 1889 set aside original allotments which numbered from one to 312. These were assigned to the people and approved by March 10, 1905. Each family head was allotted 640 acres (a section). The wife and any single person 18 years or older on July 29, 1904 received 320 acres. Each child under 18 received 160 acres. The last allotment was allotted on July 19, 1933.

In addition to the land, each allotee was also entitled to a wagon, a harness, and other equipment, as well as livestock and a small amount of cash. This was known as the Sioux Benefits. The Act of 1928 continued the Sioux Benefits to allotees when they reached the age of 18. Then in 1934, the Indian Reorganization Act also continued the Sioux Benefits to the allotees. The last Sioux Benefit of this type was issued in 1946 at

Pine Ridge. This land was held in trust by the U.S. government and could not be taxed. My parents were recipients of land and cattle.

During this period many children were kidnapped and forced to go to government schools. Their hair was cut short. They were given uniforms to wear and speaking their tribal language was forbidden. This was the government's effort to assimilate the Lakota into the white culture. The intent was to de-Indianize the children thereby forcing them into white society. No longer did the families live close together under the immediate supervision of the chiefs. The families built log cabins along the creeks and began to live almost like white people. They raised small herds of horses and cattle.

Today, the Lakota tribal groups are governed by elected tribal councils. Many Lakota have left the reservation and now live in urban areas. The Rosebud Lakota Tribe has a university, and other tribal groups have four year colleges on their reservations. Some of the tribes have developed casinos to generate income. The Lakota tribal groups remain among the poorest American Indians in per capita income. Today, members of the Lakota nation are scattered across the nation, but there are concentrations of Lakota on fifteen reservations and Indian communities. They are listed below:

- Pine Ridge
- Rosebud
- Cheyenne River
- Standing Rock
- Sisseton
- Yankton in South Dakota
- Devils Lake, North Dakota
- Santee, Nebraska
- Crow Creek
- Lower Brule
- Flandreau in South Dakota
- Fort Peck in Montana
- Upper Sioux
- Lower Sioux
- Prairie Island, Minnesota.

Today the approximate population of the Lakota stands at 90,000.

On July 23, 1980, in *United States versus Sioux Nation of Indians*, the U. S. Supreme Court decided in favor of the Lakota. The Supreme Court ruled that the Black Hills were illegally taken and that remuneration plus interest was to be paid in the amount of 106 million dollars. The Lakota tribe declined to accept this settlement, and the settlement remains in a trust fund today in the amount of 757 million dollars. The Lakota refused to accept the settlement because in their view it would validate the U. S. theft of their most sacred lands. The Lakota want the Black Hills back.

The history of the entire Lakota nation would be a huge volume since each of the three divisions had different experiences with the advancing whites. This narrative addresses only the Lakota, not the Nakota or Dakota.

## Spirituality and Religious Traditions and Practices

Although the philosophies and spiritual practices of each American Indian group or tribe are different, there is a thread of consistency, or a sameness, among many of these practices. Each American Indian group has its own tribal mythology, or cosmology, which describes its origin, explains the genesis of the cosmos, including the earth in its myriad of live forms, and provides models for modern behavior. Mythology, or cosmology, is a mirror of and a map for the culture that believes in and practices it. Therefore, mythology may be defined as a great body of truth for the people who believe it. Mythology explains the relationship of the people to the cosmos. Some people prefer the word cosmology to the term mythology. Having respect and love for life, the Creator of life, and those that have lived before are important features of American Indian spirituality. The whole religion is like a preparation or path to the good land, or the path of the ancestors. All have to go through it. Each day American Indian people thank the Creator for this life.

American Indians know that they can never leave nature, as it is a part of them, and they are a part of nature. When the Indian stands in the early dawn praying to the Great Spirit (the great mystery) in humility, it is an acknowledgement of the importance of being and staying in balance and in harmony with nature. The great mystery, or life force, is acknowledged in all creatures of nature, including the rocks and mountains.

This emphasis on balance is central to all tribal spiritual practices. Balance is another way of viewing harmony with one's environment, whether it involves family, friends, community, work place, school, or the animal kingdom. This leads to respect for nature and all living creatures. Rocks and rivers are considered living entities and, therefore, are respected. Animals taken for food are considered sacred and are thanked and blessed before taking their life for consumption.

American Indians place great value on the symbiotic relationship between themselves and the earth. They believe that "We are the land. More than remembered, the Earth is the mind of the people as we are the mind of the earth. The land is not an image in our eyes but rather it is as truly an integral aspect of our being as we are of its being." The inter-relatedness between people and the place they live is seen as a complete organism. Everything affects everything else. To understand American Indians, it becomes necessary to see into their complexity. This organism includes the living, as well as the inert, as seen in American Indian stories describing the Earth Mother and the Sky Father. The oral literatures of numerous American Indian groups pair the earth with the sky. Frequently, they are addressed as 'mother' and 'father' to express a family connection among parts of the visible universe.

## Environmental Issues

American Indians know how to take excellent care of the earth, unlike the dominant segment of society. Few generalizations cover all of their philosophies, but there are basic points that are relevant when contemplating the future of this planet and its limited resources. The tribes, representing various civilizations, ultimately understood their relationship with their environments. The rest of the world is finally becoming aware of the fragility of the earth and the finiteness of natural resources. American Indians are challenged with the task of preserving the environment while at the same time strengthening their sovereignty.

Another concept common to tribes is the circle. The circle has spiritual connotations of healing. The circle of life represents a view of life from infancy to death as a circle. Many tribes believe in reincarnation, thus the circle continues as the spirit reincarnates again in another human body. All ceremonies are conducted in a circle. There are prayer circles and talking circles, which are powerful spiritual healing experiences. Many Indians originally lived in circular lodges, tepees, huts, and hogans. The California Indians conducted their healing ceremonies in the round houses, which were mostly under-ground with an opening in the center of the ceiling to let in the light beams of the sun. The Lakota believe that the Great Spirit is blessing a gathering of people when the great bald eagle circles over the group three times.

The medicine wheel is another example of the circle symbolism in healing. The medicine wheel is a round circle with the four directions superimposed upon it. This is an ancient symbol used by almost all the Native people of North America and South America. There are many different ways that this basic concept is expressed: the four directions of North, East, South, and West, starting at the top of the circle and going clockwise is one of the most common methods. The North point represents mental processes, the East represents the spiritual processes, the South represents the emotions, and the West represents the physical parts of life.

The number four repeats as an important number among American Indian tribes. Other examples of the use of the number four are the four symbolic races (Black, White, Red, and Yellow). There are four physical world elements (water, fire, earth, and air). There are four worlds of existence (mineral, animal, human, and plant/vegetable). In addition, there are four dimensions of human knowledge (understanding, action, reflection, and interpretation).

Four has many important meanings to the Lakota, as well as to many other tribes. There are four ages: the age of the child; the age of adolescent; the age of the adult; and, the age of the aged. There are four entities that breathe: those that crawl; those that fly; those that are two-legged; and, those that are four-legged. There are four elements above the earth: sun; the moon; the stars; and, the planets. There are four parts to the green entities: the roots; the stems; the leaves; and, the fruits. There are four divisions of time: day; night; moon; and, year.

The Indian strives to express, in ceremony and in symbology, a reflection of four: there are four endurances in the Sweat Lodge; four direction offerings in the Pipe Ceremony; and, four direction facings in the Sun Dance. The vision questor carries four colors and places these four colors in a square within which he or she sits. Other references to the number four are the four grandfathers, the four winds, the four cardinal directions, and many other relationships can be expressed in set of four. Just like a mirror can be used to see things not normally seen (e.g., behind us or around a corner), the medicine wheel can be used to help us see or understand what we cannot quite see or understand because they are abstract ideas and not physical objects.

A relational world view, sometimes called the cyclical world view, is common to tribal cultures. It is non-time oriented, fluid, and intuitive. Balance and harmony in all relationships is the foundation of this philosophy, which includes interaction with spiritual forces. Human service workers are viewed as healers who can assist an individual in reestablishing balance among many interrelating factors in one's circle of life. Health exists only when all elements are in balance or harmony. Helpers and healers, upon entering the world of the client, manipulate the balance contextually, cognitively, emotionally, physically, and/or spiritually. An effective helper is one who has an understanding of the complex, interdependent nature of life and can utilize physical, psychological, contextual, and spiritual forces to promote harmony and balance.

Concepts of power and relationships for the Lakota include all life dimensions. Gaining or developing power, one definition of empowerment, is viewed by the Lakota as receiving help from the spiritual and natural world for a higher purpose than the individual self. This assistance is to benefit the entire Lakota Nation.

## Lakota Ceremonies

Among the Lakota people, there are a number of important ceremonies that one must become familiar with, when working with Lakota people. These traditional ceremonies are explained in this section. They include

7

Keeping of the Soul, Inipi: the Sweat Lodge Ceremony or Rite of Purification, Hanblecheyapi: Vision Quest, Wiwanyag Wachipi: The Sundance Ceremony, Hankapi: Making Relatives, Ishnata Awicalowan: Preparing a Girl for Womanhood, and Tapa Wanka Yap: Throwing the Ball. All of these ceremonies have a healing effect on the participants and are manifestations of the spiritual life of the individuals as it relates to the family, group, and community. These ceremonies are briefly describe herein:

## Keeping of the Soul

In the Lakota tradition, this was the first rite of seven given by the White Buffalo Calf Woman to the people. In this ceremony, the soul of a dead loved one is purified so it can return to the Great Spirit. The second part of the ceremony is the give-away, which takes place a year after death. All of the deceased's possessions are given away a year after the funeral. During the year, the widow or widower makes and procures gifts and decides what friends will be the recipients. The gifts are presented at a give-away dinner. It is a wonderful non-materialistic activity in the remembrance of a departed relative or friend.

## Inipi: The Sweat Lodge Ceremony or Rite of Purification

While people of the world are struggling with spirituality, spirituality has forever been an integral part of life for the American Indian; yet, the complexities of modern Western culture make observing a spiritual way increasingly difficult. The sweat ceremony is at the heart of the spiritual life of most American Indians.

This ceremony is used as a cleansing ceremony. It is part of healing and restoration. It is the mending of a broken connection between people. The participants in a ceremony say the words "all my relations", or Mitake Oyasin, before and after the prayer. These words create a relationship between humans, animals, and the land. To have health, it is necessary to keep all those relations in mind. The intention of this ceremony is to purify and heal the spirit. This healing is accomplished by a kind of inner cleansing of the inner self or re-establishing a geography of the human spirit and the rest of the world. The broken off pieces of self and the world are reunited and become whole again. Each person brings together the fragments of their lives in a sacred act of renewal, and connections are re-established with others.

This ceremony requires a structure, fire, and water. It represents the universe and connects the participants to the past, the earth, and the spiritual world. It is a place for teaching, praying, singing, purifying, and communing with others. As participants sing, pray, and enter into a trance, they believe that the ritual sweat bath purges their impurities and brings both spiritual and physical health by restoring balance. One feels renewed, reborn, and purified after participation in the ceremony. Women and men usually have separate ceremonies. Most of the American Indian residential alcohol treatment programs throughout the nation incorporate this ceremony in their programs to enhance the recovery of participants, regardless of their tribal affiliation.

## Hanblecheyapi: Vision Quest

This ceremony is usually performed on an isolated mountain top or butte and places the quester alone before the Great Mystery. The vision seeker endures a period of fasting and going without water. The vision questor prepares himself or herself in the sweat lodge before ascending to the isolated area. In cool weather or at higher elevations, a blanket or a sleeping bag is needed. This ceremony requires only the questor and four twigs with pieces of colored cloth tied to them, representing the four directions. This is an especially important ceremony for young people who are ready to face the challenges of the adult world. It is a time of reflection on their spiritual and occupational paths.

The purpose of the vision quest is not to make one's self feel important or to be interesting to one's friends, but to realize the vastness of the universe and the oneness with it. The vision quest is done for the purpose of self-improvement. It is done for a deeper insight into the why of one's being here.

## Wiwanyag Wachipe: The Sun Dance Ceremony

The Sun Dance is the annual coming together of the tribe to thank the Great Spirit for all that has been given to the people. The emphasis is on tribal unity, peace, and strength through the honor and thanksgiving offered to the Great Spirit. This ceremony lasts for four days and is usually held in late July or early August. It begins on a Thursday and ends on a Sunday. The ceremony requires a cotton wood tree, an arena, and a tribal gathering. The Sun Dance chief is usually the most respected holy man among the medicine people and one who is very knowledgeable in the traditions of the Lakota. He is responsible for the ceremonial activities and makes most major decisions during the four day event.

The men wear a kilt skirt secured by a belt around the waist, or use a woman's shawl as a dance kilt. Sage wreaths circle the dancers' wrists and ankles. Eagle feathers are placed on the head like a crown. The women sun dancers wear plain white dresses made of cloth or buckskin. The dresses are red, yellow, black, or white (tribal colors), with simple beadwork adorning them. There is no rehearsal for a Sun Dance. It is a ceremonial prayer, and like all Indian prayers, it is spontaneous.

## Hunkapi: Making Relatives

The purpose of this ceremony is to create a bond between people that is closer than a kinship tie. The ritual is for friends to adopt one another into a new relationship. The exchange or gift of a peace pipe, or a special stone, can symbolize the spiritual blood bond that occurs here.

## Ishnata Awicalowan: Preparing A Girl for Womanhood

This ritual recognized the importance of women as the source of the flowering tree of the Lakota nation. The ceremony is a source of much holiness for the women and for the entire Lakota nation. It is also known as a rite of puberty.

## Tapa Wanka Yap: Throwing the Ball

In the ceremony, a small girl stands at the center of the circle and throws a ball from the center outward to the four quarters of the universe, symbolizing that the Great Spirit is everywhere. The ceremony establishes the relationship of the people to the universe, or to the Great Spirit, who is everywhere.

# Humor and Coyote, The Trickster

Humor, in general, has traditionally been a key aspect of some tribal cultures. Vine Deloria (1969) points out that "the humorous side of Indian life" is lacking in American consciousness. The Lakota people are exactly opposite of the popular stereotype. They can find humor in the most dire situations. When a people can laugh at themselves and laugh at others and hold all aspects of life together without letting anybody drive them to extremes, then it seems that these people can survive (Deloria as cited in Trout, 1999). Humor is a feature of the Trickster, an important American Indian entity, often personified as the coyote. The trickster is comic in the sense that he does not reclaim idealistic ethics, but survives as a part of the natural world; he represents a spiritual balance in a comic drama, rather than the romantic elimination of human contradictions and evil.

The coyote is found in many trickster stories of California Indians, specifically in the story told by the Maidu Indians, wherein Coyote seems to have brought mischief into a perfect world. In fact, he brings tears and death: that is he brings uniquely human emotions and the reality of the end of life, without which there cannot be human life as we know it. Trickster stories are told to American Indian children for the purpose of teaching moral, spiritual, and religious principles. The moral and religious importance of Trickster myths and cycles cannot be ignored. It has been argued that the funny and immoral activities of the Trickster are used to teach children morality by negative example, but the most important function of the American Indian Trickster, in general, is to mediate between the human world and the divine, to call attention to the element of disorder (even death) that makes the world real and alive, and like the earth goddesses of some mythologies, to teach humans how to survive.

Many Lakota people, like my parents, integrated Christianity with traditional Lakota practices. They were converted to Christianity through the boarding school experience and lived their lives blending both belief systems when possible.

## References

DeLoria, V., Jr.(1969). *Custer Died For Your Sins: An Indian Manifesto.* Toronto: The Macmillan Company.

DuBray, W.(2001). *Spirituality and Healing: A Multicultural Perspective.* Lincoln, NE: Writers Club Press an imprint of iUniverse, Inc.

McGaa, E. (1989). *Mother Earth Spirituality.* New York: Harper Collins.

Trout, L. (1999). *Native American Literature: An Anthology.* Lincolnwood, IL: NTC Contemporary Publishing Group, Inc.

# Chapter 2

## My Family History

My mother was born in 1891, and my father was born in 1883. Both were Lakota and were born on the Rosebud Lakota reservation at a time of great conflict and danger for their very survival. The Lakota tribe was fighting with the U. S. government for food, shelter, and land, and they were losing the battle.

After my mother's entire family was starved to death she went to live with her mother's sister. My mother was a small child at the time and remained with the maternal aunt until her teenage years when she traveled to the Carlyle Indian School in Pennsylvania. She stayed at Carlyle until she was 22 years of age, and then she returned to the Rosebud reservation. She had one brother who died of starvation with her parents. My maternal great grandmother was a spiritual healer who used herbs and plants in healing. My maternal grandfather was of English descent.

At Carlyle my mother was out placed in wealthy homes as a maid and/or kitchen helper. She learned to cook, to sew, to wash and iron cloths, and to run a household. She met and married my father shortly after returning home from Carlyle. My mother was a very serene person, always smiling and usually optimistic about life in general. She sewed quilts and was a wonderful cook and pastry maker. She baked bread and pastries every week including cinnamon rolls, sweet rolls, and pies which were her specialty. My mother spoke English and three dialects of Lakota.

My father had five siblings and many step siblings. His father had married four Lakota women, and my grandmother was his fourth and last wife. My grandfather was a French fur trader who was originally from Quebec. He traveled to St. Louis and later to the Dakota Territory.

My father attended a Jesuit boarding school until the fourth grade when he ran away due to the cruelty of the nuns and brothers who ran the school. He had learned to read and write and knew basic mathematics when he left the school, never to return. For most of his life he read continually and was self educated through reading books on history and newspapers, which kept him well informed and successful in raising a large family of ten children. He was a horseman who was skilled at riding broncos and breaking wild horses. In his early adulthood he drove cattle from the Texas area to the Dakota Territory, living on the open range. When he married my mother, she was 22, and he was 31 years of age.

My father was a very intelligent man with spiritual gifts similar to that of a medicine man. He made predictions of events to occur in the future with great accuracy. He was a quiet man of few words, but spoke with authority. He played the violin and spoke several languages. He was a very serious person for the most part and profound in his speech. He was a strict disciplinarian and was definitely the head of the household.

The young couple moved to my mother's allotted land, and they built a log cabin and proceeded to farm the land and raise horses, cows, chickens, and geese. The area where they settled was called the extended reservation. My father plowed the land with a team of horses and planted corn, barley, wheat, and alfalfa. My parents also planted a large garden with potatoes, melons, tomatoes, carrots, turnips, parsnips, lettuce, onions, radishes, cucumbers, and cantaloupes. My mother picked wild blackberries, choke cherries, plums, and buffalo berries to make jams and jelly.

On this farm they reared ten children, three sons and seven daughters, and they lived on this farm until the end of their lives. The log house was built down in a valley to protect it from the strong winds that blow across the prairies of South Dakota during the summer in thunder storms and during the winter in snow storms and blizzards. The house was built near a spring that supplied water for drinking and irrigation for the garden, as well as water for the livestock. The house was surrounded by large elm and cottonwood trees that provided shade during the hot summer months.

During the 45 years of their marriage, the house did not have indoor plumbing or electricity. We read by the light of a kerosene lamp. A wood stove was used for heating and cooking for the first 30 years, until an oil heater was purchased to heat the house, and a gas stove was purchased for cooking and baking. They did not have a telephone. A battery operated radio was their main contact with the outside world. The house was one half mile from a main highway where their mail was delivered to a metal mail box five days a week. They were surrounded by other farmers, several living within a mile or two.

My family was poor in material goods but rich in love and fellowship. Most of our neighbors were of Irish, German, and Scandinavian ethnicity and were farmers in similar circumstances. This was rural South Dakota, and little has changed since then. My father drove a Chevrolet sedan until he became legally blind from cataracts in his later years. After he could no longer drive a car, he depended upon neighbors to transport him to town when needed.

I was the ninth of ten children. My oldest brother was Harry (deceased); then in descending order there was Myrtle, Emma, Alvina, Lily Bernice (deceased), Leona, Kenneth, Delbert, me, and my younger sister, Violet. We are all about three years apart. My older brother and sisters had left home by the time I was born. My mother delivered her nine children at home with the help of a midwife. Only my younger sister was born in a hospital.

We were taught to be compassionate, generous, loyal, and honest and to honor marriage and family. Our family gathers every two years for a family reunion, and usually about 100 people attend. My siblings are scattered over many states, including South Dakota, Minnesota, Florida, Arizona, and California.

My parents were not perfect but on a scale of one to ten, I would rate them at 9.9. My brothers became a farmer, a carpenter, and a truck driver respectively. My sisters became a social worker, a secretary, an LVN, a nurse's aid, and a housekeeper. All are in fairly good health, and three of my sisters are in their nineties.

My parents had many challenges before I was born. My oldest sister, Myrtle, as a child caught her dress on fire while sitting near the wood stove and was badly burned on her upper legs. She spent almost a year in the hospital. My father had no health insurance and had to sell his land allotment to pay the hospital bill. During that year, my parents took turns staying with my sister in the hospital while the other parent took care of the three other children at home. My sister, Lily, died at age two of a brain tumor, and this was a source of grief and pain for the family. Overall, my siblings were pretty healthy as were my parents. They had to be, to survive the severe winters in South Dakota.

During the Great Depression, my parents were better off than most people because they raised most of their own food. They had beef, chickens, milk, and cream, as well as a huge garden of vegetables. They carried water to the garden for irrigation during the hot dry months and were able to raise enough vegetables to feed their large family. They were self sufficient for the most part and were always hard workers who taught their children to work in the garden as well.

My parents gathered dry wood in the summer and sawed it up for the wood stoves and for the long cold winters for heating. My father had huge hay stacks for food for the cattle and horses during the winter months. The fall was a time to winterize the log cabin and lay up food in the cellar for the winter. Potatoes, carrots and tomatoes were stored in the cellar and kept fresh throughout the winter. The cellar was also a safe place to go during severe wind storms in the summer months.

# Chapter 3

# The Early Years of Childhood

I was born on April 22, 1932, on my mother's birthday. I was the typical disease model. I was born at home with the assistance of a neighbor who served as a midwife. I suffered from asthma and eczema from infancy until around age ten. This was very strange since no one else in my family had asthma. Cold air and all sorts of plant pollen would bring on an asthma attack. I grew up thinking I was very unhealthy. I could not play outside a lot of the time, if it was cold or windy. I remember spending a lot of time looking out the window watching my brothers and sisters playing in the snow in the winter time. I missed many days of school in the winter due to my asthma. The teacher would send my books and assignments home with my brother each week, and I would study independently at home.

My mother would rise at six in the morning to fix breakfast of oatmeal and pancakes. Her pancakes were the best I have ever eaten. They were very thin and almost like crepes. She also made potato onion soup with milk for us to take to school for lunch in the winter She poured it in a quart jar with a tight lid. At school we placed it in a pot of boiling water to heat it for lunch. She also made up our lunches of peanut butter sandwiches and included an apple for dessert. My father would be out milking the cows before breakfast. When I reached eight years of age I also helped milk the cows before breakfast. We would separate the milk, feed the calves, and then come in for breakfast.

I lived three miles from school, which was a one room school house with only six to eight students. I was the only person in my grade, so I had a tutor in grades one through eight. I could go as fast or as slow as

I wanted and, thus, received an excellent education in the basic skills of reading and mathematics. The one limitation was that our poor school district had little funds to buy new books. The library was sparsely stocked with very little fiction. Very few of the great books of literature were available. Most of the books were non-fiction basic textbooks, encyclopedias, and reference books.

My older brother Delbert and younger sister, Violet, and I would usually walk the three miles to school. Sometimes we rode horses but mostly walked. It took us about one hour to get there, and in the winter we were very cold when we arrived at school. The teacher lived at the school. She would have a nice warm fire going in the large furnace, so we huddled around it to get warm. We took our lunch, peanut butter or bologna sandwiches, and usually cream of potato or onion soup. We heated our soup in jars that we inserted in a large kettle of hot water boiling on a hot plate.

One day my brother, Delbert, and I were on our way to school riding double on our saddle horse called Ginger. Ginger was an experienced saddle horse and was always a safe horse to ride. There was one section of the road to the schoolhouse where we had to ride on the highway due to a steep embankment on both sides of the road. As we were riding on the highway a neighbor drove up behind us in his car and tooted his horn. Ginger leaped into the air with fright and took off running. I was thrown off and landed on the highway in front of the car. The impact knocked me unconscious. When I awakened I saw two men leaning over me asking me if I was "okay". I hurt all over, especially in my chest. I still had the handle of my syrup pail lunch bucket in my hand. The impact separated the handle from the pail. My brother was able to stay on Ginger even though the horse ran two miles before my brother could calm Ginger down.

The two men, neighboring ranchers, took me home. I think I might have broken or cracked several ribs. We did not seek medical treatment as I was able to walk and appeared to be normal to my parents. I stayed home a couple of weeks to recuperate. I have never been on a horse since that day.

I have always loved school and found the studies to be very easy. I loved my teacher, a widow in her fifties, who had a real dedication to teaching. She was my favorite teacher and taught us for several years. I would help her by cleaning the blackboards and by dusting the erasers during recess. I think she felt sorry that I could not play with the other children when it was windy due to the pollen in the air and my asthma.

My mother always baked bread on Tuesday. She was a wonderful cook and made several loaves at a time. She also would bake sweet buns and cinnamon rolls. When we came home from school we always looked forward to having a snack of cinnamon rolls and coffee with a lot of cream. My mother was a wonderful mother. She was orphaned as a child and was raised by a maternal aunt. She attended Carlyle Indian School until she was twenty-two years of age. She was very conservative in dress, wearing only navy blue, brown and black dresses. She never wore long pants as that was not the style then. She had long black hair which she braided and wore in a bun in the back. She was a devoted wife and mother. She never smoked cigarettes or drank alcohol. She never wore makeup or permed her hair. My mother was the heart and soul of our family. Her love and attention made her children feel loved and important.

My mother had a mellow personality, very serene and peaceful. She liked to laugh and smiled a lot. She took great pride in her cooking and was a gourmet cook. She had learned to cook while working in wealthy homes in an out placement program at Carlyle.

Because of my childhood asthma, I spent a lot of days indoors when the weather was cold, often missing school. My asthma was not medically treated. My parents learned that cold air was a trigger for my asthma, and I would start wheezing. My parents, therefore, kept me indoors for most of the winter months. I remember standing at the living room window watching my brothers and sisters playing in the snow. I could not play outside, and I missed out on the building of snowmen, sledding, and other winter activities. I believe that childhood illnesses play a major part in the development of our personality. Illnesses create dependency and a lack of mastery—two challenges that I had to overcome.

My father, I believe was clinically depressed. He would be withdrawn sometimes for weeks at a time. His depression was not severe enough to immobilize him, as he always rose early in the morning and was very self disciplined. He worked every day, unless he was physically ill, which was seldom. He was irritable at times, and we as children, never knew what kind of mood he was going to be in. We walked on egg shells when he was depressed, so as not to cause any more stress in the family. He was a good provider for the family and was very protective of his children. We were not allowed to spend the night with friends because he was concerned that someone might harm us. I believe he may have been abused by the Catholic nuns in school and did not want that to happen to his children.

My father suffered from an enlarged heart, which was probably a leaky valve from birth. His health problems did not interfere with his work, because he worked when he did not feel well. My father took his responsibility for his large family very seriously and did the best he could.

My younger sister and I liked to sing. We would look forward to the Christmas program at school where we usually sang the Christmas carols together. My father would help me with my homework. He also liked to sing a song called the "Big Rock Candy Mountain". He sang when he was not struggling with depression. He always took us to the school for our annual Christmas program.

I remember a hot August day on our farm in South Dakota. The sky was clear with a few cirrus clouds on the horizon. Father Gall had just driven down the dusty road leading to our log cabin from the main highway. The priest would come to teach us catechism, hear confessions, and administer mass the next day. He would usually spend the night and leave after mass the next morning. Father Gall was an immigrant priest from Germany and spoke with a heavy brogue. He had been assigned to St. Francis Indian School for the last thirty years and seemed to enjoy it. Father Gall served the Lakota living on the extended Rosebud Reservation and those Lakota who lived on farms and ranches. They were the Lakota farmers like my parents living in remote areas Father Gall's monthly visits were usually on schedule, with him spending the night as our guest during the winter months, when the church would be too cold in sub-zero for us to meet there. During the summer months he would spend the night at the small church twelve miles north of our farm, but, today was an exception.

Why had Father Gall come today? He had a special treat for us because this was the last week before the start of school, and it was time for my younger sister, Violet, and I to pick out our school cloths from the boxes of used clothing he carried in the trunk of his car. We tried on numerous coats to find one that was not too long and not too small. We giggled as we paraded around the front yard in our new coats. There were also sweaters, stockings, and dresses to pick from. Next week we would go in to town to pick out our school supplies and new shoes. I especially liked to buy a new pencil box with all of the little compartments for erasers and pencils. We would buy new shoes with space for growth. Our old shoes were pretty worn out with holes in the soles replaced with card board. We put a lot of mileage on our shoes, as we walked six miles a day back and forth to school.

On this particular day my mother was preparing dinner of fried chicken, mashed potatoes, with gravy, fresh sliced tomatoes from our garden, and an apple pie, freshly baked for the priest. Earlier in the day, Violet and I caught two roosters, and helped prepare them for cooking. My mother butchered them and prepared them for frying/baking.

My father came in from the field with his team of horses. He removed the harnesses from the horses and watched the horses roll on the ground as they finished a long day of confinement pulling the farm equipment or hay wagons. The horses would prance to the water tanks to drink the cool well water running from the natural springs under the beautiful elm trees. Here it was cool and shaded from the hot sun. The horses looked forward to a well deserved rest after a long day.

My father was tired, too; one could see it in his walk. He rose every day at sunrise to milk cows, separate the cream from the milk in a machine, feed the calves, and eat breakfast, and then he harnessed up the horses for another long day of working in the fields. After dinner he milked the cows, separated the milk, and fed the calves. Even though he suffered from a chronic heart condition, I never heard him complain. On this day, my father washed up at the well and joined the priest and our family for a delicious mid-western dinner.

I remember once in the middle of winter a blizzard came up while we were at school. My father harnessed up the team of horses and drove the wagon to the school to get us and bring us home. He was worried that we would get lost in the storm. and he was a very loving and protective father. He had blankets that he wrapped around us, and we snuggled together in the wagon as we traveled the three miles home. I have always known that my parents loved us children dearly and would sacrifice all for our welfare.

We were taught that families are forever. One's family will always love you and help you when you need help regardless of what you have done. One's family will forgive you and continue to love you unconditionally.

# Chapter 4

## The Formative Years

When I started high school in a nearby town, I was an honor student. My education in a one room schoolhouse had served me well. I had developed good study habits and was ahead of most of the town's teenagers in basic skills. I developed friendships with three girls who grew up on farms. We remain friends to this day. All three of my girlfriends married farmers. They all live on farms in South Dakota.

In school, I loved meeting new people and participated in the music program, first playing the French horn and later the baritone horn in the marching band. I also worked on the school paper, sang in the school chorus, and played girls basketball. During my junior year, I began working in a small sandwich shop during lunch time and after school. Meeting the public was a new experience, and it was my first job. I spent most of my earnings on cloths.

During my freshman year, I stayed with some friends of my family and later lived with my older sister Alvina. I slept on the couch in the living room of her small house. During my junior year, I stayed with my aunt, Josephine. She was my favorite aunt, and she was always cheerful and optimistic. In my senior year, I rented a room in the home of friends of my family who were retired farmers. My high school years were some of the happiest years of my life. I was moderately popular and very inner directed. I did not smoke, drink, or have sexual relationships. I also did not associate with students who liked to party. I had an undying love for learning. When I daydreamed, I saw myself living far away from South Dakota in a warmer climate.

My first boyfriend was a Catholic boy who was very religious. He attended mass daily, and his brother was a priest. We dated for about two years, going to dances and movies. He was more like a big brother than a boyfriend. He was three years older and was an average student. He later married one of my girlfriends and became an accountant.

I wanted to go to college but I knew my family could not afford it. At that time there were no community colleges in South Dakota or financial aid programs, such as the PELL grant or student loans, and I would have had to attend a state university which cost more than we could afford.

As a young adult I realized that I wanted to live in town. I did not like living on the farm because it was too isolated. I also liked city life better than milking cows, feeding chickens, and working in the garden. I decided that I would definitely never date or marry a farmer. I am sure my asthma had something to do with this decision. Farmers spend a lot of time outdoors with exposure to dust and pollen which I could not tolerate.

While working in the sandwich shop I met my future husband. He would come in for afternoon coffee and was a friendly person to visit with. He was Norwegian, good looking, and six feet tall. He was working for the postal service and was five years older than me. He was also a pilot and owned a small plane with a friend. We would go flying on weekends and fly out to my parent's ranch. We would circle the farm house and land about a mile away on a flat grassy area. My family would drive up to pick us up. We would also go flying to other cities for shopping trips. We also liked to dance and attend movies. He taught me how to drive a car when I was sixteen.

We married a year after we met. I was only seventeen years of age, and he was twenty-two. I was a senior in high school. One of my best friends married at about the same time. We graduated high school as married women and became young mothers. Within two years we had two children, a boy named David and a daughter named Yvonne. I was mature for my age, and I was a very protective mother to my children. I stayed at home, cooked, and kept house just like my mother had taught me.

We discussed going to college, but we had to wait until after the Korean War, because he was called to active duty when our first child was only six weeks old. He was stationed in Colorado Springs,

Colorado where I joined him for the first year. He was then assigned to Elmendorf Air Force Base near Anchorage, Alaska. We relocated to Alaska by driving up to Alaska on the Alcan Highway through western Canada, which was a ten-day trip during the month of November. The road was snow packed, and all one could see was snow and pine trees for the ten days.

Although we had a lot of friends in the military, I did not enjoy my stay in Alaska. I was pregnant with my daughter and gave birth at the air force hospital at Elmendorf. The winters were long, and there was very little sunshine. The snow never melted. We played cards with other young couples for entertainment. I was happy to return home to South Dakota after a year. We took a train to Juneau, then boarded a large naval ship to sail to Seattle, where we picked up our first new car, a 1952 Plymouth sedan. We traveled back to South Dakota via California and made a vacation out of our trip.

Upon returning to South Dakota, we decided that we would make plans to go to college. When David was five years old and Yvonne was three, we moved to Vermillion, South Dakota so my husband could attend the university. He would get his Doctorate degree in Optometry, and I would attend college later. In the meantime, I had to go to work to help support the family. He had the GI Bill educational benefits which helped pay for tuition and books.

The next five years were a struggle financially. After two years at Vermillion we moved to Memphis, Tennessee so my husband could attend Southern College of Optometry. I went to work as a bookkeeper in a small insurance office, and we hired African American women to provide child care when we needed it. The south was a totally different culture. Everything was segregated in 1957. We joined the Methodist Church and made friends with other couples who were also students.

During the time we lived in Memphis, both of my parents passed away. My parents were up in years. By this time my father was 74, and my mother was 68. They had worked hard most of their lives and now they would rest in peace. After their passing, South Dakota never seemed like home anymore.

We began to plan a move to California after my husband graduated in 1960. I was excited about moving to California after living in a large city, South Dakota seemed too rural and too cold for us.

I became pregnant with my third child, a boy that we named Lester. He was born in California after we settled into our new home in Antioch. Antioch was a small town of 17,000 in a heavily populated county adjacent to San Francisco. It was an ideal town to raise a family in, but it had a fast growing population. My husband went into private practice and dearly loved his work.

We joined a church, and I returned to work to help support the family while my husband built up his clientele. I worked as an accountant for a large corporation for the next four years until our finances allowed me to be a homemaker once again. Life was busy with three children, their activities, little league, piano lessons, swimming lessons, summer camp, and all that goes along with raising a young family.

We became active in the church. I directed the choir, and we taught Sunday school and had a large group of church friends. We took vacations in Yosemite, Santa Cruz, the Redwoods, Disneyland, and day trips to Golden Gate Park in San Francisco. My husband and I joined singing groups and performed the Messiah every year. Everything seemed to be going great. We bought three new homes, moving up to bigger and better homes. Our last home had five bedroom, two bath, and two stories. The home also had a swimming pool and a jacuzzi.

I decided it was time for me to return to college and enjoyed every minute of the college experience. College opened up a whole new world to me. I started out majoring in music, but then switched to psychology with plans to enter the mental health field.

After my daughter was the victim of a violent crime at the hands of four boys under the age of eighteen I was drawn to psychology. From this event in my daughter's life, it became a struggle to maintain my own sanity. The attackers were given probation, and none of them served any time in jail. I was angry, revengeful, depressed, confused, and concerned about my daughter's recovery. She saw psychiatrists and other counselors, but nothing seemed to effectively help her heal from the trauma. She became addicted to drugs to kill the mental anguish, and her life spiraled downward.

I was full of anger and wanted to get revenge. I carried around this anger for many months. Finally, I sought counseling and was able to give up my pursuit of getting revenge. In the meantime my family was falling apart.

My husband became depressed and our marriage came to an end after thirty years. It seems that he fell into a black hole and could not get out. The man I loved and admired became a shell of who he once was.

We got a divorce, sold the beautiful home we once enjoyed, and moved on with our lives. Marriage takes work and commitment. Honesty, trust, and common values were no longer present in our relationship. The divorce, however, did not crumble my future. I was finishing my doctoral dissertation at the time my marriage ended. This painful event helped me realize my own spiritual strength for survival in the times of deep sadness. Life exists within all of us and not in the external. It is not the events in life that are important but how we respond to these events. The human spirit is strong and can endure of unspeakable pain, and yet be victorious in its own ability to heal itself.

Divorce brought me pain and tears as well as newfound confidence and peace. Divorce is an event involving tremendous grief When our cherished dream falls apart it is difficult to realize that life has many lovely discoveries waiting for us, even on the other side of a broken heart.

# Chapter 5

## Work and Teaching

I started back to college at age 37. My two older children were out of the house adults, and my youngest child, Les, was nine years old. I started out by enrolling in a community college fulltime. My first grade report was all A's. I dearly loved college, and everything seemed so easy and enjoyable.

I finished my AA degree and transferred to San Francisco State University for my Bachelors of Art (BA) in Social Science Interdisciplinary studies. I then received a Masters degree in Social Work (MSW) and later enrolled in a Doctoral program in Educational Psychology at the University of San Francisco. I received my Doctorate in 1983. I was licensed as a clinical social worker (LCSW) in 1976 and had a private practice since that time.

During these years, I met many interesting people, and the university opened many new doors for me. While in the MSW program at San Francisco State University, several of my professors became my mentors and encouraged me to teach as a lecturer. I accepted a position as Director of Social Services at a non-profit multi-service agency in Oakland, California which entailed supervising twelve employees. I had completed an internship at this agency in the second year of my masters program and was excited to accept this new challenge.

This was an opportunity to work in administration and develop some new skills. I began to write proposals for additional funding. My first proposal for a nutrition program was accepted and funded by the federal government for $200,000. The program involved consumer buying clubs, nutrition education and cooking classes. I included a free lunch program served Monday through Friday to 25 homeless and low income people at our agency. We purchased a new dishwasher, pots and pans, dishes, and cooking utensils, and we hired a cook to purchase the food and prepare the lunches.

Our agency provided social services to thousands of American Indians from numerous tribes. We provided mental health services, crises intervention, youth recreational activities, a ladies club, and court advocacy. The agency had many community meetings. I recall meetings with Caesar Chavez, who spoke about the struggles of farm workers, and Buffy St. Marie, who played her guitar and sang folk songs. I also recall that Dennis Banks and his wife attended some of our fund raisers for the agency. It was a very exciting time in the history of civil rights, and our nation was struggling with many opposing factions fighting to be heard.

While working in this agency, I began to see the need for mental health workers of American Indian ancestry to meet the needs of the thousands of clients we were serving. My staff consisted of paraprofessionals who needed to have advanced training to more adequately serve the American Indian clients. The services offered in most mental health programs were not relevant to the needs of these American Indian clients. Most mental health workers did not understand the cultural uniqueness of American Indians and the diversity of their tribal beliefs and practices. Many of our tribal people suffered from intergenerational trauma resulting from generations of mistreatment by the government.

After I had worked at the agency for two years I decided to collaborate with a mentor at San Francisco State University to develop a training program for American Indians at the BA and MSW levels. The program would offer funds for the students for tuition, books, and living expenses. We submitted the proposal to the National Institute of Mental Health in Washington, D. C. The project was funded for five years and was to be housed at San Francisco State University. I was hired to coordinate this project and began recruiting students.

We recruited 32 students and offered special classes that addressed American Indian culture. Students also were mainstreamed into the regular curriculum of the university. They were mostly BA level students who later entered the MSW program. This program was very successful and provided personnel for agencies in the surrounding area.

We also offered annual human service conferences to present workshops to the hundreds of American Indian paraprofessionals working in the agencies in the San Francisco Bay area. We invited nationally known guest speakers and local professionals to lead workshops.

While teaching at San Francisco State University, I began to develop curriculum that could be used in schools of social work throughout the United States. The courses I taught were Group Therapy, Social Casework, Social Work Practice, Ethnic Cultural Content, Psychopathology, Human Behavior and the Social Environment, Advanced Social Work Practice, American Indian Psychology, and Spirituality and Social Work. Later I was graduate advisor for master's thesis for second year students master's level students in social work. I also fostered an environment conducive to fellowship among our students and faculty.

After twelve years of teaching, I left the university to direct a program in Santa Rosa, California. This was a behavioral health program connected with a medical clinic. Here I supervised a staff of six. We provided basic mental health services to thousands of American Indian clients with emotional problems and crises situations. We developed a youth organization to provide tutoring and sports activities for youth who were at high risk of dropping out of school. The program was very effective, and parents were happy to become involved in their children's activities. We provided field trips, a six week summer youth program, and health screening through our medical clinic. We also provided court advocacy for clients in trouble with the law. We worked closely with protective services in child welfare cases and, in many instances conducted, home studies and made recommendations to the county for disposition of the court cases.

After four years as Director of this program I was recruited by the Department of Health and Human Service (DHHS), Public Health Service (PHS), Indian Health Service to become Chief of Human Services for the state of California. This position involved extensive travel at the national and state levels. I coordinated 39 alcohol rehabilitation programs (eight were inpatient), 19 mental health programs, six social service programs, and eight urban medical clinics. The medical clinics were in Los Angeles, Santa Barbara, San Diego, Fresno, Bakersfield, Oakland, San Francisco, and Sacramento.

The clinics provided comprehensive health care including medical, dental, substance abuse counseling, mental health services, health education, and, outreach services. My duties were to evaluate these programs and provide quality assurance, staff recruitment, funding, licensing assistance, and administration assistance. All programs were evaluated annually.

I also evaluated mental health programs in other parts of the United States that were funded by the U. S. government. In California after successfully assisting the mental health programs in licensing their staff, I felt that it was time to return to academia. I accepted a tenure track position at California State University, Sacramento in 1990.

At California State University, Sacramento I assumed the position of Chair of the Mental Health Concentration within the Division of Social Work. Having lectured at San Francisco State University, University of California Berkeley, and Los Medanos College, it seemed like I was coming home. I had extensive clinical and administrative experience that needed to be shared with social work students who would potentially be working with American Indian clients or who were American Indian themselves.

I continued to develop curriculum and publish books and articles in professional journals. I also submitted another proposal for training American Indian students, and this proposal was funded by the National Institute of Mental Health.

Most of my writing has addressed services to American Indians. I have always felt it helpful to collaborate with other faculty of color in publishing ethnic cultural content My Doctoral Dissertation was a comparative study of cultural values of American Indian social workers and Anglo American social workers at the master's level. My findings supported the significant differences in values between these two groups.

While teaching at California State University Sacramento, I submitted a proposal in collaboration with other social work programs in the state for student stipends for child welfare workers. This program was funded and has brought in millions of dollars to the campus to support the education of MSW students interested in child welfare work, including a number of American Indian students. This proposal was funded under Title XX of the Social Security Act.

Another interest of mine has been transpersonal psychology. At California State University Sacramento I developed an elective course on Social Work and Spirituality. This was a very rewarding course to teach, and the students seemed to enjoy it very much. This course addresses the part that the spiritual life plays in the development of the personality of the client. I collaborated with several faculty members in editing a text book for the course entitled, *Spirituality and Healing a Multicultural Perspective.* Some of my books and journal article publications are:

DuBray, W. (1978, Fall). Grief Counseling with Native Americans. *White Cloud Journal of American Indians and Alaskan Native Mental Health, (1),* 2.

DuBray, W. (1980, October). The Indian Woman and Her Family. *Social Casework.*

DuBray, W., Eisenbisc, M., & Cress, E. (1978). Human Behavior and American Indians.

DuBray, W., Purcell, F., & Cress, E. (1980). Social Policy and American Indians.

DuBray, W. (1980). Cultural Values: An Assessment and Comparison of Value Orientations of Anglo American and American Indian Social Workers. Ann Arbor, MI. University Microfilms International.

DuBray, W. (1981). Grief Counseling. In Richard Dana (Ed.). *Human Services for Cultural Minorities.* San Francisco, CA: University Press

DuBray, W. (1982). A Descriptive Bibliography on Human Behavior and American Indians. In *A Source Book in Child Welfare: A Descriptive Bibliography on Racial Ethnic Groups.* Ann Arbor, MI: University of Michigan School of Social Work National Child Welfare Training Center.

DuBray, W., Cress, E. (1983). The Urban Indian. San Francisco, CA: San Francisco State University.

DuBray, W., Eisenbise, M., & Cress, E. (1983). Social Work: Methods of Intervention with American Indians.

DuBray, W. (1985). American Indian Values: A Critical Factor in Social Casework. *Social Casework.*

DuBray, W., & Larsen, I. (1990). *Domestic Violence Handbook for American Indians.* Sacramento, CA: Indian Health Services.

DuBray, W. (1991). The Role of Social Work Education for Indian Child Welfare. In *Developing Linkages for the Future: Indian Child Welfare and Schools of Social Work.* Tulsa: OK: University of Oklahoma School of Social Work and Three Feathers Associates.

DuBray, W. (1992). *Human Services and American Indians.* St. Paul, MN: West Educational Publishing.

DuBray, W. (1992). California's Homeless American Indians. *Humboldt Journal of Social Relations.* Humboldt, CA: California State University, Humboldt.

DuBray, W. (1993). *Mental Health Interventions with People of Color.* St. Paul, MN: West Publishing.

DuBray, W. (1995). Lakota Ways. In C. James, *Catch the Whisper of the Wind.* Health Communications, Inc.

DuBray, W. (1998). *Human Services and American Indians,* (2nd ed.). Belmont, CA: Brooks/Cole Publishing, ITP.

DuBray, W., & Sanders, A. (1999). Interaction Between American Indian Ethnicity and Health Care. *Journal of Health and Social Policy.*

DuBray, W. (1999). *Mental Health Intervention with People of Color,* (2nd ed.). Belmont, CA: Wadsworth.

DuBray, W. (2001). *Spirituality and Social Work.* Lincoln, NB: Writers Club Press, iUniverse.

DuBray, W., & Sanders, A. (2003). Values Orientation/ Worldview Framework. In J. Anderson and R. Carter (Eds.), *Perspectives for Social Work Practice.* San Francisco: Allyn and Bacon.

DuBray, W. (2003). Integrated Services in American Indian Country. In J. Dworkin (Ed.). *Advanced Social Work Practice.* San Francisco: Allyn and Bacon.

In addition to publishing, I also supervised graduate social work students with their research projects required for completion of the MSW. The following is a list of some of the projects:

- Adolescent Suicide
- "Armonia": A Dropout Prevention Program
- An Assessment of Elementary Teachers
- An Assessment of Mental Health Services
- A Bereavement Program for Children
- Bilingual Interpreters in Social Work
- Care Costs for HIV Orphans
- Child Abuse Prevention Laws
- Clozapine: An Atypical Neuroleptic
- A Coming Out Handbook for Gay Fathers
- Culturally Sensitive Social Work Practice
- Cycles of Re-hospitalization and Support Services
- A Descriptive Survey of Substance Abuse Programs
- Domestic Violence among AFDC Recipients
- Domestic Violence among Asian Pacific Women
- Drug, Alcohol and Tobacco Education
- Effective Case Management of Homeless Clients
- Effects on Therapists Working with Terminal Clients
- Federal Housing Policy 1934-1992

- Fragmentation of Services to the Homeless
- Gay Community Resource Guide
- Helping Clients Cope with Generalized Anxiety
- Homeless Mentally Ill Women: Services
- Homeless School Age Children: After School Program
- Latchkey Children: Their Needs
- Lesbians Contextual Response to Intern Interventions
- A Model of Existential Social Work
- Multiple Marginality and Mexican Americans
- Needs Assessment for an Intertribal Community
- A Phenomenological Study of Widows
- Profile of Homeless Women Utilizing Services
- Resource Guide for African Americans
- A Resource Guide for the Filipino Community
- Restoring California Tribes to Federal Recognition
- Short-term Crisis Residential Program Evaluation
- Social Welfare Services to the Hmong Community
- Spirituality in Clinical Social Work
- Assessment of Registered Nurses in Hospital Social Work
- Survey of Licensed Clinical Social Workers in Hospitals
- Treatment of Gay Male Couples
- Why Do They Stay": Women and Domestic Violence
- The Wintu Intensive Treatment Program in CYA
- Foster Care as a Risk Factor in Predicting Homelessness
- BSW Internship Satisfaction
- Adolescent Fathers: A Latino Perspective
- Asian American Mental Health
- Sacramento City School Head Start
- True Identity: A Study of Racism
- Spirituality in Foster Parenting
- African-American Male/Justice
- The Black Church as a Social Agency
- Successful Iu-Mien High School Students
- Caregivers of the Mentally Ill
- Attitudes of Nurses Towards the Mentally Ill
- Resource Guide for the Hmong community
- Critical Incident Stress Debriefings
- Asian Women and Domestic Violence

- Social Services for American Indians
- Treatment of Latency Aged Children
- Minority Youth in Group Home Care
- African Americans and Foster Care
- Effects of Stress on Family Caregivers
- Resource Directory for African Americans
- Experiences of Southeast Asian Refugees
- Psychological Effects of HIV and AIDS
- Spirituality and Alcoholism Treatment

All of these projects are on file in the library at California State University Sacramento and are available for review.

## Consultation

An important part of academic appointments is to provide one's expertise to public agencies. I spent many hours as a consultant to agencies in Washington, D. C. and for other agencies throughout the country. The following is a list of some of the agencies I consulted with:

- Department of Health and Human Services, Social Security Administration, Baltimore, Maryland
- Minority Health Professions Foundation, Silver Spring, Maryland
- National Institute of Mental Health, Rockville, Maryland
- Department of Health and Human Services, Public Health Services, Indian Health Service, Rockville, Maryland
- Department of Health and Human Services, Administration for Children, Youth and Families, Head Start, Washington, D. C.
- Winnebego Mental Health Services, Macy, Nebraska
- NASW, California Chapter, Sacramento, California
- Governors Office, State of California, Sacramento, California
- National Cancer Institute, Bethesda, Maryland
- Alameda County Mental Health Services, Oakland, California
- California Department of Mental Health, LaMesa, California
- Council on Social Work Education, Aging Minorities, New York, New York

- University of California, Medical Center, San Francisco, California
- Office of Samoan Affairs, San Francisco, California
- Asian Incorporated Consulting Firm, San Francisco, California
- California Rural Indian Health Board, Sacramento, California
- Sacramento Urban Indian Health Project, Sacramento, California
- California Urban Indian Health Board, Sacramento, California
- Families In Society, Journal, Milwaukee, Wisconsin
- Advancement of Health Education, Reston, Virginia

# Papers Presented at Conferences

Over the years, I presented at enumerable conferences. The following is a list of some of my presentations:

1979 "Mental Health Services for Urban Indian Children", Department of Social Services. State of California, Multicultural Conference, Sacramento, California

1980 "Multicultural Issues in the Delivery of Mental Health Services" University of San Francisco

1980 "Cultural Conflict of Urban Indians in Continuing Care" Multicultural Conference, Region IX, Health Education and Welfare, Sacramento, California

1981 "Training Child Welfare Workers for Relevant Services for American Indian Families", National Conference on Social Welfare, San Francisco, California

1981 "Burn Out and Stress Management", Human Service Conference, San Francisco State University. Funded by National Institute of Mental Health

1981 "Research and Development of American Indian Curriculum in Social Work Education", CSWE Annual Program, Louisville, Kentucky

1983    "Impact of Divorce on Children", Divorced Catholics, Fremont, California

1983    "American Indian Cultural Values", National Indian Education Association Conference, San Jose, California

1983    "Dream Analysis", Six Weekly Sessions, Parents Without Partners, Fremont, California

1985    "Slowing Down the Aging Process", Simply Friends Single Group, Santa Rosa, California

1986    "Substance Abuse and the American Indian Patient", Indian Health Services Conference, Asilomar, California

1987    "Suicide, Depression and Crises Intervention", Annual Mental Health Conference, Indian Health Services, Reno, Nevada.

1988    "Alcoholism and Human Sexuality", National School of Indian Alcoholism, American Indian Training Institute, Sacramento, California

1988    "Symptoms of Suicide", Suicide Symposium for American Indian Mental Health and Alcohol Counselors, Westerbeke Ranch, Sonoma, California

1989    "Traditional Healing and American Indians", Traditional Health Conference in San Diego, California, sponsored by the California Urban Indian Health Board, Sacramento, California

1990    "AIDS and Suicide", Quarterly Meeting of Alcohol Coordinators of Indian Health Service Funded Programs in California, Sacramento, California

1990   "American Indian Children with Special Needs", National Indian Child Welfare Conference at University of California, Los Angeles, Los Angeles, California

1990   "Trends in Substance Abuse Treatment for the Nineties", Annual Meeting of Mental Health, Social Services and Alcohol Counselors, Indian Health Services, Santa Rosa, California

1990   "The Role of Schools of Social Work Education and American Indian Child Welfare", University of Oklahoma, Conference on Child Welfare, Oklahoma City, Oklahoma

1990   "Native American Families and AIDS Issues", American Indian AIDS Institute, San Francisco, California

1991   "Dual Diagnosed Homeless American Indians in Urban Areas", Annual Program Meeting, Council on Social Work Education, New Orleans, Louisiana.

1991   "Talking Circle Group Presentation", Sacramento Urban Indian Health Project, Sacramento, California

1991   "What, Me A Leader", A Six Hour Workshop on Leadership Skills for Indian Women, Fourth Annual Conference for American Indian Women, Sacramento, California

1991   "Mental Health Concepts", Eight Hour Workshop for Community Health Representatives from Forty American Indian Programs in the Western United States, California Rural Indian Health Board, Sacramento, California

1992   "Providing Expert Testimony in Indian Child Welfare Custody Cases", Annual Program Meeting of the Council on Social Work Education, Kansas City, Kansas.

1992   "Social Policy Issues of American Indians in California", Panel Presentation at NASW, Legislative Days, Sacramento, California

1992   "Intercultural Counseling and Psychotherapy", Winnebago Counseling Center and the University of South Dakota Conference, Sioux City, Iowa.

1992   "Multicultural Issues in Substance Abuse", Conference on Addiction Medicine and Treatment and HIV Disease, Texas Southern University, Houston, Texas.

1992   "Women and AIDS", Presentation on Family Values as Taught by American Indian Elders, at Sacramento Urban Indian Health Project, Sacramento, sponsored by California Rural Indian Health Board, Sacramento, California

1993   "Community Relations and the American Indian Faculty and Staff", Symposium on the Status of American Indians in the California State University System, Long Beach, California

1993   "Teaching Social Work Practice in American Indian Communities", CSWE, APM, New York, New York

1993   "Perspectives of Women of Color on Social Work and Social Work Education", CSWE, APM, New York, New York

1993   "Meet the Authors" CSWE, APM, New York, New York

1993   "Culturally Competent Practice", Conference on Women, Children and Families, s California State University, Fresno, Fresno, California

1993   "Positive Role Models—Faculty of Color", Panel Presentation at California State University, Sacramento,

Multicultural Student Leadership Conference, Sacramento, California

1993 "Health and American Indian Women", Conference on Women of Color and Health, University of Maryland, Eastern Shore, Baltimore, Maryland.

1993 "American Indians in 1993", Keynote Speech, Honor of Indigenous People, California State University, Sacramento, Sacramento, California.

1993 "Cultural Competence and Mental Health", Workshop on Mental Health Services to American Indians, California State Department of Mental Health, Riverside, California

1994 "Racial and Ethnic Identity at the Cutting Edge", Panel Presentation, CSWE Annual Program Atlanta, Georgia.

1994 "Meet the Authors", CSWE, APM, Atlanta, Georgia

1994 Curriculum Consultant/Speaker to the International Conference of Indigenous People and Social Work in Kamloops, British Columbia, sponsored by the University of Ottawa and the Royal Commission of Canada.

1994 Invited by the Council on Social Work Education Accreditation Commission to serve on an evaluation team to evaluate the social work program at the University of Minnesota, Duluth Campus. Prepared a written report for the Commission

1995 "American Indian Faculty and Staff in the California State University System", National American Indian Education Conference at California State University, Long Beach, California

1995 "Understanding and Dealing with Mental Health Issues of American Indian Elders", National American Indian

Geriatric Leadership Conference, University of North Dakota, Grand Forks, North Dakota.

1995 "Interactions Between Ethnicity, Family and Health Care", National Conference on Children, Youth and Families, Center for Children with Chronic Illness and Disability, University of Minnesota, Duluth, Minnesota

## Leadership Activities

As part of social work education, and as a social work educator, contributing to the leadership of the field is essential. In these efforts, I have engaged in numerous activities that leave a lasting contribution to leadership in my discipline. I have provided a list of some of these efforts:

1977-1985: Served in the House of Delegates, Council on Social Work Education, American Indian Caucus

1980-1981: Served on the Monitoring Action Committee, Department of Mental Health, State of California, Advisory to the State Mental Health Director

1981: Invited by the Reagan Administration, Department of Health and Human Services as one of 20 American Indian Scholars to give input on program development for American Indians.

1984-1987: Served on the Traditional Health Committee of American Indians in California, sponsored by the California Rural Indian Health Board

1988: Chaired the American Indian Caucus of the State AIDS People of Color Conference in Sacramento, California

1989:       Appointed by Dr. Ken Kizer, Director, Department of Health for the State of California to serve on a committee of the AIDS Leadership Committee. Duties were to develop a five year plan to address AIDS in California. A 140 page report was prepared and presented to the Governor and the State Assembly and Senate.

1989:       Represented Region IX, Health and Human Services in a workshop on Runaway and Homeless Youth at the National AIDS update Conference in San Francisco, California

1990-1991:  Invited by DHHS, PHS, Office of Minority Health to review proposals, Rockville, Maryland.

1991:       Served as President of American Indian Social Work Educators in Schools of Social Work affiliated with the Council on Social Work Education.

1991:       Served on Proposal Review Panel for Sacramento County, reviewing AIDS proposals from community based organizations.

1991:       Served on Proposal Review Panel for DHHS, PHS Indian Health Service, Rockville, Maryland, for Tribal Management grants.

1992:       Served on Proposal Review Panel for DHHS, Social Security Administration, Baltimore, Maryland for Cooperative Agreements and Demonstration Programs for the Aged, Blind and Disabled.

1992:       Served as member of the Advisory Board to the Association for the Advancement of Health Education, a national organization funded to develop culturally sensitive AIDS educational material, Reston, Virginia.

1992:      Served on a review panel for National Institute of Mental Health to review training proposals in Nursing, Psychiatry, Psychology and Social Work, Rockville, Maryland.

1992:      Nominated to the Pilot Executive Leadership Development Program, a statewide program of the California State University system.

1993:      Elected President of the Association of American Indian Social Workers of California.

1994:      Appointed to the Board of Directors of the Mental Health Association of Sacramento County.

1994:      Appointed to the American Indian Health Policy Advisory Panel for the Department of Health Services for the State of California

1994:      Served on the Program Committee for the 1995 CSWE Annual Program Meeting in San Diego, California

1997:      Served on a review panel for Administration on Children, Youth and Families, DHHS, Washington, D. C.

## Expert Testimony in Child Welfare Cases

Another area of interest for me was conducting assessments of American Indian child welfare cases. I would then prepare written reports and expert testimony to the juvenile courts in these cases. My recommendations were usually followed, and only two cases were appealed. My recommendations were followed in both of these cases. I was involved in more than 100 cases in three counties in California.

I believe that social workers play a very important role in Indian child welfare services. They are the chief investigators, and often possess the most pertinent information in the disposition of these cases. The following section discusses the Indian Child Welfare Act and problems in its implementation.

# Indian Child Welfare

## <u>Introduction</u>

There is a common misconception that child welfare agencies throughout the United States are staffed with personnel holding masters degrees in social work with a specialty in child welfare. In a national survey conducted recently it was found that very few states required any professional qualifications of their child welfare workers (Samantrai, 1987). In twenty states there was no legal mandate for any minimum qualifications. Five states required a college degree with any major. Another five states required a college degree with a social work major or training and course work in other behavioral sciences; only one state required social work licensure. MSW degrees for some specific positions were required in four other states.

California requires that 50 percent of the professional staff providing emergency response services, and 100 percent of the supervisors of such staff in child welfare, possess a master's degree in social work or its equivalent in education and/or experience as certified by the State Personnel Board (California DSS Manual-SS, 1988).

In spite of few legal sanctions in many states requiring a master's in social work as the appropriate degree for supervision and delivery of child welfare services, the contribution of social work education continues to be a major force in the provision of quality services. In addition, social work education still plays a major role in preparing social workers to assist in the implementation of the Indian Child Welfare Act.

## Indian Child Welfare Services

Social work education can play a major role in the recruitment and education of American Indian child welfare workers, as well as aiding in the implementation of the Indian Child Welfare Act throughout the United States. Before this topic is addressed, however, it is important to review the historical antecedents of present day child welfare services related to American Indian populations.

## Historical Review

The training and educational needs in the field of Indian Child Welfare can be traced to many years of federal policy designed to defeat tribalism and the conquering and Christianizing of American Indians with the goal of assimilation into the dominant American society. Historically, American Indian families were chased westward and were either captured or killed in the process of colonization. From 1830 to 1870 the federal policy was to exterminate Indians, which later changed to segregation of Indians by placing them on reservations (Unger, 1977).

A tremendous assault on Indians took place by 1875 when Indian children in large numbers were placed in boarding schools. The purpose forcing Indian children into Indian Boarding schools was to de-culturize, or de-Indianize, and separate Indian children from their parents to destroy tribal life. During these years of forced acculturation, traditional tribal parenting was disturbed and, in some instances, destroyed. The inter-generational effect of the boarding school era is still considered one of the major factors in the breakdown of Indian family traditions and has had a major impact on parenting practices for generations (Cross, 1986; Hull, 1982; Fischler, 1985).

By the 1930s, with the passage of the Indian Reorganization Act, a radical move took place to protect and strengthen the tribal rights to exist. At this time Indian parents were writing letters, to Congress and the President of the United States, complaining about the removal of children and their placement in military type boarding schools. Some children spent as many as fifteen years in these institutions if they were shipped long distances from home. From the 1950s to the 1960s the Child Welfare League of America was contracting with the Bureau of Indian Affairs in carrying out the adoption of thousands of Indian children to non-Indian families. Racism was the catalyst for these widespread adoptions and foster placements of Indians into non-Indian homes where these children became non-persons. They were raised in white homes but were never accepted by whites socially as appropriate candidates for dating or marriage to white partners. These children had no connection to their own culture and were rejected by the white culture. Later, as adults, they developed mental health problems and substance abuse problems as they searched for an Indian identity and a positive self-image. In the 1950s the federal policies toward Indians emphasized termination of tribes, relocation to cities, and assimilation of Indians into society as a means of destruction of the tribal cultures.

## Indian Child Welfare Act

In 1967, the Association on American Indian Affairs in New York began investigations into the frequency of placement of Indians into non-Indian homes. The rates of non-Indian placement varied from 25% in some tribes to 100% in other tribes. While the Indian child welfare investigations commenced in 1967, changes to the care and placement of Indian children were not quickly accepted. After eleven years of investigations and congressional hearings the bill, the Indian Child Welfare, authored by James Abourezk, Senator from South Dakota, was signed into law in 1978. Every part of the Act addresses specific problems existing in Indian country. The heart of the law is in the intention of keeping Indian children with their families and within the Indian community. There is no other law like this law in the United States. The law regards tribal culture and customs as of paramount importance. The law is an attempt to tip the balance in court proceedings in favor of the tribes.

Although the law has been established law since 1978, the law has been poorly implemented due to:

1. Insufficient funding levels for tribal programs;
2. The failure of federal and state agencies to implement adequate programs for Indian parents and families;
3. Continued unlawful practices by state child protection services toward Indians;, and,
4. A lack of emphasis on the Indian Child Welfare Act in the education of social workers throughout the country.

## The 1990s

Today, hundreds of years after the trauma of wars of resistance, relocation, and forced acculturation in boarding schools, the inter-generational scars can be clearly observed as a major factor in the social, spiritual, and emotional problems present in Indian country. Many Indian people are searching for their cultural identity as they come in conflict with the values of a dominant society which places materialism, competition, and greed for power as the top priorities of the day. Racism remains the underlying dynamic in many practices toward American Indians as Indians stand between the land and those who want more land (DuBray, 1985).

There are many unmet needs within the Indian communities for relevant mental health services for youth and families. There is a need for treatment and healing of adults and children who have been physically and sexually abused in federally funded boarding schools. There are unmet needs for effective treatment for substance abusers who demonstrate high rates as victims of child abuse. Furthermore, there is a need for parenting skills for those descendants of the boarding school era. In addition, there is a great need for culturally sensitive child welfare services. Finally, there is a need for assistance in community development as tribes move toward addressing problems of substance abuse and domestic violence from a community approach. The schools of social work education can assist American Indians in many areas by linking with tribal programs and through the recruitment of Indian students interested in a social work career.

## Indian Child Welfare Services and the Roles of Social Workers.

Social workers are involved in all aspects of Indian child welfare including protective services, removal, placement, and adoptions. With the growth of social service protective services and the development of advocacy roles, many social workers are spending more of their time preparing court documents. Family evaluations are increasing because court cases on children and parents are increasing. It is no longer sufficient to just establish neglect or abuse; the "right" to treatment and rehabilitation requires social workers to be actively involved.

The needs of the court dictate the extent to which any one social worker plays the role alone or jointly with others. The following are five major roles of social workers in the courts.

1.  Petitioner: A petition to remove the child from his/her parents under mandate of the "society's interest" to protect children through court action is customarily filed by the social worker.
2.  Defendant: The social worker may have to answer charges for an agency that is being sued and also occasionally may be named personally as a co-defendant. An example would be a suit by a foster parent requesting the court to restrain the agency and the social workers from removing the child.
3.  Expert witness: Because of his/her knowledge and experience in child welfare, a social worker may appear on behalf of a child or parent for very specific issues.
4.  Client Advocate: A social worker may explain the problems of the child or parent to justify behavior(s) or to place in needed services.
5.  Resource: The social worker functions as a resource of the court staff to aid in fact-finding and treatment and is then responsible for court report(s) upon which a disposition is based.

## Role Conflicts of Social Workers

According to the National Indian Justice Center in Petaluma, California, the following problem areas concern social workers:

-   Social workers often do not know the rules on due process and the difference between facts and hearsay. As a result, they are reluctant to be cross-examined in court, particularly to have the social services report be treated as evidence.

-   Social workers dislike resolving problems by adversary techniques. Social workers would generally rather resolve problems by case conferences and consensus.

- Social workers find it difficult to accept lawyers' demands for facts, evidence, and emphasis on sanction, authority, and law.

- Social workers feel that lawyers tend to split hairs to establish facts and tend to "place" blame and faults thus leaving little room for reconciliation; social workers feel that lawyers will "advocate" for their clients, right or wrong.

- Many times social workers see judges as "advocates" for the parent causing the social worker to prepare reports "in defense" of the child. This places the social worker in the position of appearing to be "against the parents."

- Social workers may be unsure of when to terminate an informal relationship with the parents and when a case should be filed in court, as well as what legal position the parents should have. Consequently, they may have problems concerning their role with the family and the family's perception of that role: Friend or prosecutor?

- Social workers feel that lawyers see them as emotional do-gooders who are over-identified with the clients' problems.

- Social workers may have difficulty establishing sound legal basis for their recommendations.

- Because federal employees are not subject to tribal jurisdiction, BIA social workers are not required to carry out the tribal court orders; this presents limitations for tribal courts.

- Social workers are uncertain about "immunity" and responsibility for "liabilities." When a public agency is specifically required to carry out a protective function for children, the public agency can be held legally responsible (liable) for non-performance. The direct service worker is given the responsibility to perform. Does this mean "removal of children from their parents," or "returning children to their parents"? In every case, the front line social worker must make the decision: Either decision is subject to challenge.

- When there is no required public agency, the responsibility to perform depends solely on the professional ethics of the front line social workers. Immunity for these workers is usually unclear, hampering the ability of the social worker to make sound decisions.

- There are serious jurisdictional problems and conflicts in many communities concerning the division of roles and responsibilities between the BIA, the tribe, and the state social services.

- In many communities, there are problems concerning the division of roles and responsibilities between law enforcement and social services.

- The role problems for social workers become more complex when the social worker has to also function as the advocate for the petitioner in court hearings.

- The social worker is the central role in child abuse and neglect cases, and they must interact with all of the others involved in these cases. Consequently, they have the greatest potential for role problems and must work diligently to develop good working relationships with the other professionals involved in child abuse and neglect cases.

- These issues need to be addressed in social work education in courses such as Social Work and the Law.

## Training Needs Assessment

In response to a survey conducted in 1990 by Three Feathers Associates and the University of Oklahoma, School of Social Work several training needs have been identified by Indian child welfare programs as the top ten worker skill area. These skill areas are still needed today. These skill areas are as follow, listed in ranked order by percent of responses:

Training Needs:

> Sexually abusing families
> Teaching parenting skills
> Providing culturally sensitive services
> Foster parent's role with biological parents
> Working with involuntary clients
> Psychological and social processes of separation
> Preventive outreach to families at risk
> Documentation for court proceedings
> Working with physically abusive families
> Treating troubled families

In addition to the above, the greatest personal training needs in supervisory knowledge are as follows, which are also listed by ranked order by percentage of responses:

Training Needs:

> Measure service outcomes
> Conflict resolution in the work group
> Plan and implement staff development programs
> Evaluate workers performance
> Time Management
> Grant writing
> Develop community resources
> Retention of trained staff
> Facilitation of supervisory conferences
> Stress management

In view of the information gained in this survey it is hoped that curriculum will be forthcoming in the form of teaching modules specifically addressing these needs. Teaching modules could be shared on a national level through affiliation with the Council on Social Work Education and at annual meetings.

## Recruitment of American Indian Students

There is a great shortage of American Indian social workers nationwide. Even today. American Indian social work students usually make up less than one percent of masters level students and even fewer in the number of doctoral students. Schools of social work should more actively recruit American Indian students and provide financial aid such as the Title XX of the Social Security Act. The Indian Health Service and the BIA should fund the education of American Indian social work students at both the BSW and MSW levels.

## Implementation of the Indian Child Welfare Act

Schools of social work can play an important part in assisting in the implementation of the law by providing comprehensive education about the Act and raising the issues about implementation in the college classroom. In addition schools of social work can provide planned part-time MSW programs for staff employed in Indian Child Welfare Agencies who are in need of graduate education. Classes and weekend seminars can be brought to remote areas by closed circuit television and traveling faculty when there is a strong commitment to social work education. California State University, Sacramento has provided a Children and Family program of this nature in northern California.

Schools of social work can also provide seminars for Children's Protective Service Departments in county programs where the law is poorly implemented. There are no limits to the assistance schools of social work can provide when faculty are concerned about implementation of the law. The challenge then is to educate faculty of schools of social work on the importance of emphasizing the Indian Child Welfare Act in all concentrations within the social work major and provide curriculum to complete the task.

The faculty, of schools of social work, need to conduct research on effective interventions with abusive families. There is also a need for curriculum which better prepares social workers to function in the many roles required in managing child abuse cases involving the courts.

## Summary

Social work education can play an important role in preparing child welfare workers to staff agencies serving American Indian families, by recruitment of American Indian students and inclusion of the Indian Child Welfare Act as a basic part of the curriculum for all concentrations within the major and by developing linkages with tribal and urban based American Indian child welfare agencies. In addition, schools of social work can sponsor conferences, symposiums and in-service training to county child welfare agencies and federal agencies responsible for child welfare services to American Indian communities. Social work educators can develop Indian Child Welfare teaching modules and curriculum which can be utilized nationwide to aid in implementing the law. Social work education can provide advocacy for Indian populations by scholarly publications in national and regional journals, as well as providing expert testimony in critical court cases where due process is questioned. It is hoped that by improving the education of a new generation of social workers, the Indian Child Welfare Act of 1978 will move toward implementation and American Indian tribes will again have jurisdiction over Indian child welfare matters.

## References

California Department of Social Services manual, (1988)

(1987). Child Abuse and Neglect. Petaluma, CA: Legal Education Series, National Indian Justice Center.

Cross, T. L. (1986) Drawing on Cultural Tradition in Indian Child Welfare Practice. *Social Casework, 67,* 283-289.

DuBray, W. (1985). American Indian Values: Critical Factor in Casework. *Social Casework,* 30-37.

Fischler, R. S. (1985). Child Abuse and Neglect in American Indian Communities. *Child Abuse and Neglect, 9* (1), 95-106.

Hull, G. H. (1982). Child Welfare Services to Native Americans. *Social Casework, 63*, 340-347.

Samantrai, K. (1987). Unpublished Dissertation. Los Angeles, CA: University of Southern California.

Unger, S. (1977). *The Destruction of American Indian Families*. New York: Association on American Indian Affairs: New York.

# Chapter 6

## Parenting

The most challenging experience of my life has been that of parenting. Not that it is unpleasant or unrewarding, but because so much of our own identity is bound up in the development and experiences of our children.

In a way, we learn so many lessons of life through this experience. We grow as individuals as we join in that eternal partnership with each of our children. Each child has his/her own personality that we respond to sometimes positively and, unfortunately, sometimes negatively. So much of our behavior is unconscious, and we are unaware that many of our decisions regarding our children stem from our own narcissism.

Our unresolved conflicts (we all have them) tend to find resolution or become more problematic in the act of parenting. I was fortunate to have had a loving mature mother as a role model in parenting, yet each family is unique in the personalities involved. I was also fortunate in having a happy life while growing up in my teen years, a period when some children get lost and involve themselves in impulsive and destructive behaviors. I was inner directed as a young teenager and was given much freedom to make personal decisions while going away to school in the ninth grade. I saw no need to rebel against the teaching of my parents. When my mother said, "do not drink, smoke, or have sex", I followed her direction and have lived seventy-eight years without smoking and avoiding alcohol until I was in my fifties (then drinking sparsely), and I have never had promiscuous sex.

When our children are hurting, we tend to blame ourselves as having some parental deficiency. A psychologist once said that we, as parents, are as happy as our most unhappy child. We empathize with whatever feelings our children are going through, and we are joyful when they are joyful and sad when they are sad.

In looking back at my parenting practices, I could have been less of a disciplinarian and should have been more patient and understanding in many instances. Since I became a parent at age 17, and had two children by the time I was 19, I was very young to assume such responsibilities. Their father was a better parent then me, and I am thankful for that.

My father was very strict, and my mother was the mellow, nurturing parent. When faced with problems of parenting I would think about my own parents and follow what I thought they would have done in similar circumstances. Fortunately, my children were all born in good health and above average in intelligence. I can empathize with parents who have children with severe birth defects and autism which will try the patience of even the most mature and loving parent.

One of the common situations I find in our society is that children are short changed when parents are struggling to survive in our society. Due to poverty, parental illness, or family conflict, many children are caught up in family crises not of their making. In my experience, my children and I sacrificed greatly in helping their father attend college and receive his doctorate. I believe that they would have been better off if I had not gone to work and left them to depend upon too many babysitters.

We provided our children with a stable home life, food, shelter, and clothing and saw to it that they attended school and church activities. We exposed them to additional learning experiences such as museums, zoos, and visits to parks such as Yosemite and Yellowstone National Park, as well as Disneyland. They had swimming lessons, piano lessons, and summer church camp as part of their socialization into the community. Our children had a fairly normal childhood as the children of a couple who may have been too focused on our own education to be ideal parents.

Their father taught them how to roller skate and snow ski, and he was a scout leader with the explorer scouts. He and I both taught Sunday school, and we were both active in the church throughout the years of our marriage.

The crises of parenting came when our beautiful fifteen year old daughter was a victim of a violent crime while attending a birthday party at the home of a Baptist minister. These criminals were barely under the age of eighteen and were only given probation. This trauma destroyed the life of our daughter, and she was never able to recover. We utilized psychiatrists and other counselors, but she was never able to overcome the trauma and humiliation of the experience and her post-traumatic stress disorder (PTSD). She became addicted to drugs and alcohol and struggled for many years before her death at age 38 from advanced liver disease.

Yvonne was a gifted child with an IQ of 140. She was talented as a musician and played the piano, organ, and violin. She was also a gourmet cook and prepared all of the holiday dinners. She was a kind and loving parent, and her traumatic experience broke my heart. I miss her every day. I have never been able to get over this loss, but have learned to live with it day-by-day. She had married and given birth to two children, Angela and Joseph. I became their guardian after her death as they were both minors, and she was divorced from the father of the children. Angela developed a terminal kidney disease and died at age 21. My oldest son and his wife decided to help me raise Joseph, and he lived with them from age six until he graduated from high school and enlisted in the U. S. Air Force. He is presently stationed in Seoul, Korea having spent tours of duty in Iraq and Dubai. I will forever be indebted to my son and his wife for opening up their hearts and home to Joseph. They have one son, Peter, presently a college student. Joseph and Peter grew up as brothers because they were one year apart in age.

David, my oldest son, was active in all kinds of sports, including golf, basketball, baseball, football, and wrestling, and he was also a good student. He married Diane. and they have one son, Peter. David became a licensed electrician and an independent contractor. He had his own business in Oregon. He suffered a major heart attack at age 55 and has been disabled ever since.

My youngest son, Lester, graduated with a Master in Public Administration and presently works in the bio medical research field. He conducts clinical trials of new medicines for a large research organization. He lives in San Francisco, with his life-long soul mate, Gary.

I have tried to teach my children that family is forever. We are loyal to each other and helpful when needed. People are more important than things. Material things will fade away but relationships are forever.

I have seen my children as a blessing and a source of both joy and sorrow. I am a better more mature and compassionate person for having been their mother and learning from them. I have a loving relationship with my children, their partners, and my grandchildren. I hope that I have fulfilled my role as their mother and have given them the support, encouragement, and inspiration to live life to the fullest and the courage to fulfill their true potential in this life.

# Chapter 7

## My Legacy

Part of my legacy is to mentor young people in their career choices. I was fortunate in my career in having very generous and idealistic mentors who were humanitarian.

My first mentor was Pat Purcell a professor in the Social Work Department at San Francisco State University. He was of Irish and Norwegian ancestry and spent his early childhood and young adulthood in North Dakota. He held doctorates in psychology and in public policy. While a student at New York University, Dr. Purcell had worked in New York City as a community organizer with a large youth program. He was a brilliant group worker and knew how to get things done. Dr. Purcell had formerly been the chair of the Department of Social Work at San Francisco State University.

Dr. Purcell was my instructor in social work policy. He frequently played the devil's advocate to provoke discussion in the classroom. He helped me hone my debate skills in his classes. Dr. Purcell and I authored several books together on American Indian policy and human behavior and the social environment.

Dr. Purcell was responsible for me being recruited as a faculty member several years after I graduated with my master's degree. He and I collaborated on submitting a mental health training grant which was funded by the National Institute of Mental Health. It provided stipends for American Indian graduate and undergraduate students in the field of social work.

Dr. Purcell gave me the encouragement that I needed to pursue a teaching career. He also encouraged me to continue my education and pursue a doctorate degree which was necessary to receive tenure.

Later I was fortunate in having another mentor whose name is Ron Boltz. He was the chair of the Department of Social Work at California State University, Sacramento. Ron was of German and Lakota ancestry. He held degrees in divinity and social work. Ron was always available with a listening ear to give me encouragement and advise when needed. Ron taught statistics and research in the graduate division of social work. He steered me away from potentially dangerous paths that would ultimately have derailed my tenure possibilities.

I was hired by the Department of Social Work at California State University to chair the mental health concentration within the masters program. This program prepared social workers to work in the mental health fields. Since I had years of experience in providing direct services and in administration of mental health programs, I was well qualified to chair this concentration.

The academic field involves many mine fields that can damage one's career if the wrong path is taken. There is a considerable amount of politics and back stabbing in academia in all disciplines. Getting tenured is a challenging process, so one needs a mentor to guide one in publications and committee work in order to be successful.

My own mentoring involved, along with two American Indian colleagues, organizing American Indian Social Workers of California to encourage American Indian students to get involved in the political process in furthering causes that would help this population. I frequently organized social activities such as pot luck gatherings in order to recruit students, and I have lobbied for financial aid for students pursuing a college degree. I have also provided support and guidance to many American Indian students as they pursued their degrees.

Presently I lobby for better programs for the homeless population in Sacramento. This entails writing letters and signing petitions for improved funding for this population. Several of my former students are presently working with the homeless population in Sacramento, and much progress has been made in providing training and affordable homes for them as a temporary step for them in becoming self sufficient again. When I was teaching, I published books and articles addressing relevant approaches for working with American Indian clients and other cultural minorities. In these publications, I addressed the differences in cultural values of these populations that are not served by a white middleclass approach to their problems. Perhaps this has been my major contribution in the social work curriculum.

In looking at cultural values we are including the study of techniques, economic organization, kinship associations, government, law, religion, art, folklore, and other aspects of human culture. Ethnologists who emphasize those aspects of culture which most extensively involve relations within and among groups are often referred to as social anthropologists.

Much of the early research on American Indian values was conducted by social anthropologists using the case study approach. Some of the anthropological field studies consisted of long term observations of American Indians in their natural social environment. This involved learning the language and closely sharing their lives in order to penetrate beneath the surface to richer insights and understandings of true cultural values.

Autobiographies, biographies, and psychological analyses provided a glimpse of cultural values and individual configurations of behavior. My research focused on comparing cultural differences between Anglo American and American Indian social workers at the master's level. I found significant differences between the two groups.

## Time Orientation

Examples of cultural differences are seen in how clients perceive time in their lives. Some clients are **present time oriented**, while others are **future time oriented**, and still others are **past time oriented**. This is one area that helps us understand why people make the decisions that they do.

The mean American Indian social worker showed a relatively higher preference for a **present time orientation** in comparison to the Anglo-American social worker. This finding may be surprising as descriptive of a group of educated, financially comfortable, mental health providers. The focus of a **present time orientation** is on living from day-to-day as best as one can and enjoying life as it comes. It demonstrates an appreciation for the here and now with little focus or confidence in the future. This **present time orientation** may stem from the history of the American Indians' struggle for survival in the face of adversity. There appears to be little concern for materialistic goals or accumulation of wealth which usually motivate a **future time orientation**.

## Relational Orientation

Other areas of study were in the relationships to family, groups, and country. Individualism is popular in Caucasian cultures but not common among American Indian tribal cultures. In my research I found the mean American Indian social worker showed a tendency toward a collateral orientation in the relational category. Collateral orientation places the welfare of the group first. Many American Indian societies are focused upon an extended series of patterned kin reciprocities. About the most unfavorable moral judgment an Indian can pass on another person is to say "he acts as if he didn't have any relatives".

American Indians today are considered "undependable" in the view of some Anglo Americans primarily because Indian thought and behavior give easy priority to the collateral framework. Taking or leaving a job is not a matter for purely individual decision, but rather must be considered with the family. The Indian community is group oriented and frequently gets together to deliberate many hours before consensus is reached on policy decisions.

Family tension among American Indians often follows lines of value conflict. Indians moving to urban areas who embrace the concept of the nuclear family suffer value conflict due to isolation. One may speculate that keeping the personal business of the immediate family segregated may lead to weakening of all ties to the extended family and the wider circle of relatives. Those who have spent more time among Anglo Americans often want to introduce new ideas or to claim privileges of individual inheritance and autonomy that they discovered prevail among Anglo Americans.

The nature of authority patterns stem from this orientation. Indian people place a high value on the welfare of the extended family, and this family loyalty is sometimes mistaken for dependency. A loyalty to family and group consensus is sometimes seen as blocking the individuation process as conceptualized by some Anglo American social workers.

## Man/Nature Orientation

Another area to consider is how people relate to nature, whether they try to live in harmony with nature, seek to achieve mastery over nature, or are subjugated to nature. Most American Indians live in harmony with nature with a view that there is no real separation of man, nature, and super nature; one is simply an extension of the other, a concept of wholeness derives from their unity.

In my research, the mean American Indian social worker showed a relatively higher preference for a **harmony with nature orientation** than the mean Anglo American. The aim is to maintain "balance" or "harmony" among the various aspects of the universe.

This philosophy explains why some American Indian tribes have fought against strip mining on their lands. This mining on their lands would upset the ecology of the earth and create an imbalance of nature. Most tribes have not been impressed with the profit involved in mining silver, copper, and other metals.

The Indians understand that they are linked intimately with the earth in a network of rights and responsibilities. The earth is viewed as their mother, and the sky as their father. The land then is sacred, encompassing a spiritual dimension dating back to the Ice Age.

## Activity Orientation

The mean American Indian social worker in my research tended to chose **being** over **doing**, which implied that intrinsic worth is more important than education, status, power, or wealth. Explanations and predictions regarding American Indians can be made about important aspects of the mother-child relationship based upon their activity orientation. A preference for a **being** activity orientation, for example, can be used to make predictions as to whether a mother will be accepting of her child for what he or she is rather than what the child can accomplish as compared to the performance of siblings or the children in other families of a locally circumscribed group. This may be one of the reasons that American Indians do not push their children to excel in the educational system.

# *Chapter 8*

# The Next Generation of Native Women

It is of utmost importance for Native Women to continue to teach and inspire the next generation of women. Although the sacrifices and challenges are great, the rewards are many. I personally have never had the opportunity to be enrolled in a class with a native woman as teacher. I have received feedback from thousands of students who were impressed with my world view, my philosophy, and my value system, which is that of a Native woman.

In the years I spent teaching at three universities, I was at a disadvantage in the tenure process. I was hired with soft money from the National Institute of Mental Health, and the five years administering this grant did not count toward tenure. Many minority faculty are exploited in this manner and are at a disadvantage in comparison with other faculty. Some of our large prestigious universities are guilty of this exploitation.

The following survey conducted on the California State University system reveals other challenges that American Indian faculty face when teaching in higher education. It is extremely important for minority faculty to have mentors to guide them through the tenure process and the mine fields in academia.

## Survey

In 1994, a colleague, Dr. Morgan Otis, and I conducted a survey of American Indian faculty and staff in the California State University (CSU) system. The study was funded by the Chancellors office of the California State University system. The CSU system at that time consisted of 20 campuses throughout the state of California, employing more than 16,000 faculty and serving more than 326,000 students. The CSU system offered more than 1,500 bachelor's and master's degree programs in some 200 different subject areas. A limited number of doctoral degrees were offered in collaboration with the University of California and private institutions in California. Three of the CSU campuses had been ranked by the *U.S. News and World Report* as among the top ten percent of regional colleges and universities in the country.

Faculty salaries in the CSU system continue to attract faculty from throughout the country. The National Center for Education Statistics (NCES) conducted a study of 3,025 institutions of higher learning in 1991-92. This study stated that average faculty salaries in public institutions in California were found to be the highest in the nation. The lowest salaries in public institutions were found to be in Wyoming.

Our study intended to identify the issues and concerns of American Indian faculty and staff, in addition to collecting information on recruitment, assignments, retention, tenure, and departure from the California State University System.

## Sources of Data

Two questionnaires developed by the investigators were mailed to 151 faculty and staff members of the CSU System. Forty responses were received and formed the study sample.

## Conclusions Reached

Analysis of the data revealed that most of the respondents were male (25), were members of out of state tribes (31), and held Ph. D.'s (19). Most of the faculty respondents were tenured or were in a tenure track position. Females numbered 15. As a group they had been productive in the development and publication of 276 journal articles, 15 books, and 29 chapters in books. Most of the respondents identified other ethnic groups as faring better than they (29); however, they were for the most part satisfied with their positions (22), and planned to stay with the system until retirement.

## Faculty Responses

Of the 25 faculty responses, eight were lecturers, two were Assistant Professors, two were Associate Professors, and 13 were full professors. Fifteen of the faculty taught at both the Bachelors and Masters levels. They taught in a variety of disciplines. They held a total of 37 leadership positions. Most of the faculty, 54% of the respondents, did not feel that either the department or the university in which they worked held a serious commitment in hiring of American Indian faculty. Most of the faculty, 58% of the respondents, did not feel that their department or university had been successful in hiring American Indian faculty.

Most of the faculty, 75% of the respondents, felt that other ethnic groups fared better then they, with 62%, naming Euro-Americans as getting favored treatment over all minorities. African Americans were considered by 30% of the respondents as getting more favored treatment than American Indians, and 20% of the respondents felt that Hispanics were getting more favored treatment than American Indians, while only 4% percent indicated that Asians were getting favored treatment over American Indians.

Less than half of those responding to the survey saw the overall environment as being conducive to a pleasant work situation for American Indian faculty. Less than half, 44% of the American Indian faculty, felt their Chair or Director was supportive of them in achieving their professional goals. Less than half of the American Indian faculty, 40%, felt that the opportunity to participate in decision-making was either high or very high. Some 20% of the American Indian faculty felt that the opportunity to participate in decision-making was either low to very low to none.

The survey participants felt that the opportunities for leadership roles available to American Indian faculty, in their departments, were high or very high by 44%. Some 30% of American Indian faculty saw opportunities for leadership as low to very low to none.

The level of institutional racism in their department/programs was seen by American Indian faculty as low to very low by 37% with 12% seeing it as high to very high. The level of harassment of American Indian faculty by administration was seen as low to very low to none, by 62%.

In regard to remaining employed in the CSU system, 62% of those responding planned to remain employed in the system. This is also the same percentage of respondents who reported being tenured. One third, 33% of the faculty, had filed grievances in order to be retained, tenured, or promoted. Several respondents communicated with one of the researchers by telephone, requested to remain anonymous, and were afraid to respond in writing. These subjects were working in very hostile environments and would not identify their campus location.

The CSU system was seen as a condusive working environment by less than half of the American Indian staff and faculty. A list was developed of the eleven (11%) concerns voiced by staff and faculty. These concerns reflect alienation, lack of mentors, lack of support systems on campus (45%), lack of sensitivity regarding their culture by colleagues, and cultural value conflict in many areas.

## Implications:

The CSU system was seen as needing improvement in its recruitment and retention practices for American Indian students, staff, and faculty. American Indian faculty were discouraged from researching or writing about their own ethnic group and were penalized, while Euro-Americans were rewarded for research on their ethnic groups. This is clearly a double standard which penalizes American Indians and creates unfair criteria for tenure and promotion. American Indian journals were not recognized as refereed journals by many tenure committees which clearly discriminated against American Indian faculty who chose to write about their ethnic population and publish in American Indian journals.

American Indian faculty are very successful in bringing in funds through grant writing, but they are usually overburdened with the responsibility of managing these programs. They remain on soft money positions while their counterparts move in to tenure track positions.

Grant writing in many universities is not considered "scholarly" activity and does not carry much weight in the tenure process.

## My Philosophy

I have always felt that all people can learn, and many can do outstanding and creative acts that they did not think possible. Many students need feedback or encouragement to achieve their academic goals. They are unaware of their true potential. I have had the privilege of mentoring many talented students in my teaching career.

American Indian women are transcending many of the barriers to higher education. Their lives are changing in many ways as they become breadwinners and coequals in providing financial foundations for their families. The next chapter addresses many of the changes and challenges facing these women.

# Chapter 9

## Challenges of Native Women

Changing circumstances have created a demand for more active participation by Indian women in all phases of Indian life. Indian women are experiencing often difficult role transitions as they move from the role of homemaker to breadwinner. Case vignettes illustrate the external and internal forces affecting these changes.

The new American Indian woman is moving dramatically from the safe, protected environment of the home into the competitive arenas of politics, higher education, and administration. This chapter provides an overview of the internal and external forces acting on the American Indian woman today.

In the last two decades urban Indian women have become increasingly active in the political arena. Many sit on boards of directors, some lead their tribal councils, and many participate in advisory boards to the public schools and other non-profit agencies. The shortage of Indian men and other changing circumstances, such as increased educational opportunities, have created a demand for more active participation by Indian women in all phases of Indian life, however, the active participation of the women in positions formerly held by men is seen as emasculating by some Indian men.

This activity on the part of Indian women has many consequences. Indian men (as well as other men) may be resentful of being supervised by women and may be reluctant to serve on boards dominated by women. Indian women receive little support from men in dealing with the added pressures of administrative responsibilities in addition to everyday family demands. Additional stress is placed on the Indian family as this trend continues.

## Historical Background

Today, the American Indian woman is influenced by internal and external forces that have their antecedents in tribal history, in historical events from before and after initial contact with the European culture.

### Indian Women in a Changing Culture

Literature about Indian women living in the early 1600s and 1700s, before contact with the white settlers, is sparse. Anthropological studies are written from the perspective of the white male, wherein "native women have been referred to as drudges, beasts of burden, and other demoralizing terms." It is possible that Indian women in history were not permitted to interact with non-Indian men due to cultural constraints.

In 1935 Margaret Mead conducted a careful study of the Indian woman's role, and Mead's work is a most comprehensive guide for the student of the American Indian. Despite the deficiencies of anthropological studies from which to gain a portrayal of the early American Indian woman, it is still possible to gain enough information to recreate the status and role of the Indian woman and her activities in the pre-reservation tribal setting by reading Indian writers such as Beatrice Medicine. Because of the diversity of tribes, it is difficult to comprehensively depict the early life of Indian women. The Lakota tribe has been selected for the purpose of presenting one perspective on the Indian woman as a unique and viable person who shares a body of common experience with all women of diverse cultures.

The Lakota women were exceptionally vigorous, healthy, and active women. This author has three sisters aged 90, 92, and 94. All have outlived their spouses by ten to twenty years.

The Lakota tribe viewed the woman as someone with a peaceful heart, one who never struck out against anyone. The Lakota man regarded his wife most kindly, and the people, noticing his respect for her, were reminded of women's high place in the tribe.

When the Lakota woman consented to marriage she vowed to perform her work properly and to act in a manner that honored her husband. Two or three days after the man's proposal for marriage she might present him a pair of moccasins to reveal her willingness to become his wife. Her father and relatives, by keeping the gifts he gave them, made known their approval.

After marriage, her new husband would brush and arrange her long hair in the manner that her father had looked after her mother's hair. The Lakota wife was highly attentive to the needs of her husband, perhaps for pipe or food. She was happy taking care of the lodge for her husband, seeking only a smile of his approval.

It was the woman's role to rise at dawn and prepare food for her family. This meant carrying wood and water and building a fire. When these chores were completed, she cleaned the lodge and beaded moccasins for the family members or tanned hides for robes and lodge covers. After the evening meal the family would settle down for an evening of storytelling, teasing, and playing.

The Lakota woman, independent for the most part, played a submissive, supportive role to the husband. She could express her concerns, but he made most of the decisions affecting the family. It was customary for the Lakota husband to take additional wives, sometimes younger sisters of his wife when their husbands were killed in battle. This was functional to insuring the welfare of the extended family in times of loss of the breadwinner.

## Arrival of the White Man

By the early 1800s, white fur traders began to trade guns, beads, and alcohol to the Lakota Indians in exchange for furs. It was at this time that the breakdown of the cultural customs began. Under the damaging influence of alcohol, Indian men and women began to neglect their families and tribal responsibilities. Also, Indian women began to marry outside of the tribe, often choosing the English and French fur traders.

In 1815, the United States government coerced tribal leaders into signing treaties that they could not read, nor understand. These treaties opened the territory to homesteaders and miners, who flocked in by the hundreds and thousands. Soon after contact with the Europeans, the Indian people began to suffer a decline in health, and by mid 1800, epidemics of cholera, measles, and smallpox had wiped out many Indian villages.

## The Move to the Reservation

As the influx of whites continued to grow, eventually becoming the dominant group, Indians became restricted to reservation areas, and, by 1849, the Bureau of Indian Affairs was given full authority to oversee the activities of the Indian people. Indian families were forced to adapt to life on the reservation. This adaptation slowly destroyed a way of life that had been functional for thousands of years. The Sacred Black Hills were taken by an illegal treaty, the buffalo were destroyed for furs, and the language and religious practices were forbidden by the missionary schools and by federal law. Children were taken from their parents to be educated in the white man's mold and to begin the long process of assimilation (or genocide).

In 1887, the Dawes Act divided the reservation land into allotments, and individual ownership was given to Indians, with the idea that they were to become farmers and ranchers. The Indian men, who had lived by hunting buffalo and deer, now had to find a new way of life. No longer did the opportunity for recognition as a brave warrior or a great hunter exist. The Indian men did not even have the joy of watching his children grow to adulthood; these Indian children were strangers to them if and when they returned from the missionary boarding schools. The Indian woman suffered as well. She quietly watched her children taken from her and painfully saw the deterioration of her husband as his dreams of self-fulfillment became less and less a reality.

## The Move to the Cities

This situation continued until 1952, when Congress passed the Indian Relocation Act. The Bureau of Indian Affairs hoped to assimilate the Indians into the mainstream of the white society by encouraging them, with promises of training and jobs, to move to the cities. The Indians, like other ethnic migrants, formed their own communities in the cities for emotional support and survival. From 1952 through 1968 some 67,522 Indians (heads of households) were relocated through this direct employment program. Today, there are more Indians living in urban areas than on reservations.

Most Indian families adjusted to urban life, but at a great emotional and spiritual cost. Others could not adjust and eventually returned to the reservation even more discouraged than before. Urban Indian centers evolved out of a need for fellowship, emotional support, and a sense of community. During the last forty years, urban Indian centers have been the prime providers of social services to Indians, mainly because of Indian staffing and relevant casework services. The personnel staffing urban Indian centers, themselves often relocatees, provide a warm and friendly welcome to newly arriving Indians and provide social activities to assist them in the adjustment process.

## The Contemporary Indian Woman

The number of contemporary studies on Indian women is also scarce. Marion Gridley's *Native American Women* addresses the adjustment of Indian women in boarding schools, their alienation from their family, and their lack of employment opportunities on the reservation. Beatrice Medicine, a Lakota anthropologist, published *The Native American Woman* in 1978. This article is essential reading for anyone teaching or working with Indian women.

The lack of literature on Indian women leaves many unanswered questions. What are her aspirations, her goals, her conflicts, and her successes? It is important to the Indian community to be aware of where women are going and what impact they have in the areas of education, law, health, politics, employment, and family life, and this information is not readily available.

The aspirations of Indian women are to combine the best of two worlds, to survive, and to keep their families intact. To achieve these goals, many Indian women must enter the world of the employed, and this creates conflict by dividing loyalties between family and career. Because Indian culture is usually emphasized in the instruction of the children, the responsibility for teaching cultural traditions usually falls on the Indian woman. Day care centers run by Indians help somewhat to alleviate this problem.

A philosophy that still persists is faith in a spirit world to which Indian women turn for guidance and strength. For some women, the extended family provides a natural support system in times of crisis. Other women choose to request assistance from urban Indian centers or community mental health centers.

## Residual Persistence

Residual persistence with roots in the tribal culture can be observed in the personalities of most Indian women. Many tribal characteristics have survived and persisted in spite of strong external pressures to assimilate. The tradition of passing information orally from one generation to the next has persisted and is a commonality among all tribes. Spiritual values, generosity, autonomy, and decisions by consensus have also persisted in most tribes. The harmony of all living things and a reverence for the land underlay the basic philosophy of most Indian people. Many mannerisms that are uniquely tribal have also persisted, such as the Lakota mannerism of pointing with one's chin.

A modern thesis, put forward with some empirical findings, proposes a correlation between basic personality structure and cultural persistence. Irving Hallowell conducted a study to determine the degree of agreement or conformity existing between the observable acculturated behavior and the covert, inner life of American Indian people. An outline of post contact Chippewa culture was reconstructed based upon accounts of explorers, fur traders, missionaries, and others who had close association with the Indians in the seventeenth and eighteenth centuries. This material was supplemented by field observations and projective tests administered to adults and children.

Hallowell found "a considerable body of evidence that points to a persistent core of psychological characteristics sufficient to identify a tribal personality constellation, that is clearly discernible through all levels of acculturation yet studied." There may be disagreement in determining the elements that should be included in such a psychological inventory, but some commonalities are the following: restrained and non-demonstrative emotional bearings; a high degree of control over aggressive acts; the acceptance of pain, hardship, hunger, and frustration without voicing complaint; a dependence upon supernatural power; and, joking relationships with kinsmen as a device for relieving pressure within the group.

Other examples of residual persistence can be observed that allow Indian women to maintain unique manifestations of tribalness. For example, it was the custom for Lakota women to instruct their daughters and granddaughters in proper conduct throughout adulthood. Sons, however, were turned over to the father at the age of ten for instruction and guidance and rarely had direction from their mothers thereafter. Evidence of these practices can still be observed in Lakota families although, unfortunately, in fatherless homes the young sons are often without guidance, and mothers are reluctant to assume this responsibility for fear of creating a son with feminine mannerisms.

The values, belief systems, and parenting practices of the tribe determine the status role of women within each culture. Indian women also respond to internal and external forces within a context that is acceptable to their tribal affiliation. Not to do so creates internal conflict. When residual persistence is minimal, Indian women experience less internal conflict and role strain.

Internal and external forces acting on American Indian women today elicit varying responses. Inherent in the response to these social forces is the psychological set and the cultural value configuration of tribal affiliation and the degree of assimilation into the ambient society.

## The Emerging Personality

The psychological set for Indian women, as well as others, is dependent on historical events, genetic influences, and psychosocial development. Culture determines some personality traits and assigns the roles, as well as the expectations. For most Indian women, the woman's role is subservient to the male role; it is primarily the role of homemaker. The new Indian woman is experiencing role transition.

The Indian woman, however, still depends on her tribal affiliation for her basic identity and self-image. Because of extreme forms of discrimination toward American Indians, in some parts of this country, many Indians have had to deny their tribal affiliation to avoid suffering physical harm. The result is that some Indian women suffer from a need—or a belief—that they need to hide their identity. Other factors contributing to a negative self-image are media stereotypes that portray Indians as cruel savages or as drunken and hopeless. In many instances, Indian practices that are difficult to understand are often misinterpreted or diagnosed by the dominant society as indicators of psychopathology.

It is of utmost importance, then, for non-Indian counselors to be aware of the cultural values and traditions of the Indian client. Perhaps of equal importance is an assessment of the degree to which the client has assimilated into the dominant society.

In the process of assimilation, Indian women have accepted some of the customs of the dominant society. Assimilated Indian women prefer to consult professional counselors when they are in need of guidance rather than to turn to extended family or traditional healers. The culturally assimilated Indian woman with minimal residual persistence experiences less internal conflict and role strain.

## Case Illustrations

The following case illustrations provide a glimpse of Indian women who successfully face new challenges in a changing world. Living in a pluralistic society, they maintain their unique manifestations of tribalness. They are aware of having lost something of great value never to be replaced in the world in which they now live. They are, however, faithful guardians of what can be preserved of their cultural traditions and values.

These five women were reared on reservations and migrated to urban areas in search of a better life. They are healthy, motivated women who successfully made the transition from reservation life to urban life.

They range in age from thirty-five to sixty-five. All attended boarding schools at sometime in their lives. Each married an Indian man. They represent different tribes and educational levels. These women did not have the support of an extended family in their successful adjustment to urban life. They presently live in several states.

## Delphine

Delphine is a sixty-three-year old Lakota woman, married, and the mother of four grown children. She was the third of ten children born to Lakota parents. Her mother was orphaned at the age of nine and spent most of her life in boarding schools. Delphine's mother graduated from an Indian school at the age of twenty-one and married shortly after. She never smoked, drank, or used cosmetics. She was a devoted mother and never worked outside of the home. She converted to Catholicism in boarding school and reared her nine surviving children in that faith. Her guiding rule she lived by was, "the woman's place is in the home."

Delphine's father dropped out of school in fourth grade. He married Delphine's mother at the age of thirty. Most of his adult life was spent farming and raising Herefords on a 2,000 acre ranch. Delphine's parents remained married until death and lived on the same ranch for forty-three years.

Delphine attended boarding school, and upon graduation from high school, she attended Haskel Institute, in Lawrence, Kansas, where she majored in business and stenography. After graduation she worked for the tribal office on her reservation. There she met her future husband, a Lakota man, and moved to Minneapolis. The marriage ceremony was performed by a Lakota medicine man. Delphine and her husband were both in their late twenties at the time of their marriage. Delphine chose to work for several years before having children. The couple purchased their first home in a quiet residential neighborhood. After the birth of their first child, Delphine quit her job and assumed the role of full-time homemaker. She later became active on school committees and was a devoted mother to her children, consisting of three daughters and one son. When the youngest child started school, Delphine returned to work as a secretary for the school district. Her office position allowed her to work while the children were in school and to spend the summers at home. During the child-rearing years, the family returned several times a year to the reservation to visit family and friends and to participate in religious ceremonies. In the city their co-workers became their support system.

This was a close-knit family, with Delphine internalizing her mother's emphasis on homemaking. Delphine experienced little role conflict in arranging to work when the children were in school. She still was able to use her business training to pursue her personal goals. Delphine has continually honored her Lakota husband by remaining submissive to his leadership in the home and in the rearing of their son.

The couple purchased a twenty-acre parcel of land and built a small retirement cabin. They appear to be content in this heavily wooded area that borders a private lake. Their four children and their families are frequent visitors, and Delphine and her husband enjoy teaching the Lakota history to their grandchildren.

## Mary

Mary is a forty-six-year old Lakota woman who was orphaned at age thirteen and reared by an older sister. She was the youngest of five children. She married a Lakota man at age eighteen. They moved to an urban area in search of a better life. Mary gave birth to four children during her fifteen years of marriage, which ended with the accidental death of her husband. As a young widow with children to rear, she turned to personnel at the local urban Indian center as a support system. She accepted Aid for Parents with Dependent Children until she completed nurse's training. After graduation she was employed in private nursing for several years, and then she became interested in psychology. She is now completing work on a post-graduate degree in psychology.

Mary presently works as an administrator in a social service agency. She has supervised male social workers from her own tribe, as well as from the Southwestern tribes, although she has sensed resentment on their part in responding to a woman supervisor. Mary has been active on various community boards and experiences little conflict in asserting herself as a community leader. She did not assume an active role, however, until she became widowed. Her education has also contributed to her leadership skills along with external forces encouraging her to speak out for her clients.

Mary experiences some role conflict between career and motherhood. Sometimes her career as an administrator must take priority over her family. This is a source of deep concern for her because she is also a dedicated single parent. She is the only parent to her three children who are living at home. She frequently attends powwows and spends much of her nonworking hours with her children and grandchildren. She is a remarkably strong woman. Mary arises at 5:00 a.m. to complete homemaking chores before going to work. She frequently attends classes, which last until late evening. Her children have been trained to prepare meals and function in her absence. They are also taught to think and make decisions independently, a Lakota tradition.

## Julia

Julia is a fifty-two-year old Chippewa woman. She is separated from her husband and has two children. She attended boarding school and two years at a junior college. She relocated to the urban area under the Indian Relocation Act.

During her first years in the city, she worked as a nurse's aide until she entered a human service training program at the junior college level. Since then she has worked as a social worker and more recently as an agency director. Julia is an energetic woman with an optimistic attitude. She has been active on many boards and engages in community activities. She attends local powwows and cultural activities with enthusiasm. She has experienced some resentment from Indian men working under her supervision, but she has handled these incidents tactfully.

Julia is presently separated from her husband. Her more prestigious and higher paying job contributed to their marital problems. She has a strong sense of purpose in helping Indian people, which appears to be more gratifying to her than her marriage. Her children are college students with majors in human services. She does not acknowledge any role strain between career and motherhood. She has a positive relationship with her children.

## Juanita

Juanita is a fifty-five-year old Blackfeet woman, married, with no children. Her husband, a Chippewa, is a retired carpenter who spends most of his time doing volunteer work with the Indian elderly. Juanita has worked for twenty-five years as a bookkeeper in an Indian arts and crafts center. Their support system has been the personnel from the local urban Indian center. Juanita has held a homemaker role combined with an office career.

Juanita and her husband attend all powwows and Indian cultural affairs. Trips to their reservation in Minnesota have been taken on an annual basis. In this way ties are maintained with relatives and friends. They have spent twenty-five years in an urban area and are undecided about where they will live when they retire. They have been active in Indian bowling and athletic leagues over the years, and these leagues have also served as a support system.

## Kathy

Kathy is a thirty-five-year old Creek and the mother of three children. She is now separated from her Choctaw husband. She was raised in a foster home before moving to the urban area. Kathy worked as a bookkeeper before attending college, where she majored in social work. After graduating, Kathy was accepted into law school. Kathy then separated from her husband. Her pursuit of a career created problems in her marriage. Her choice was to pursue her career even if it meant the dissolution of the marriage.

She became active in the Red Nations' Women Society and the American Indian Movement. Kathy sees herself as a leader in the Indian community with the specific mission of assisting Indians with legal problems.

Kathy's support system has been personnel from a local urban Indian center. Kathy experiences role strain as a single parent. She utilizes day care facilities and other support services for her children.

## Summary

It can be seen from these illustrations that some Indian women are preparing for leadership roles, and others are actively filling those roles. Culture is a significant factor in accepting the assignment of the female role of homemaker and in providing the cause for a leadership role. Education is important to provide options for Indian women to the traditional homemaker role, or in conjunction with the homemaker role.

The National Institute of Mental Health has provided funding for Indian social work projects throughout the United States. These projects provide stipends for students in undergraduate and graduate studies. For example, San Francisco State University's Department of Social Work was awarded a five-year training program. Federally funded programs such as this one provide recruitment, financial support, and encouragement to Indian women seeking to fulfill their potential.

## Conclusion

Indian women demonstrate a resilience and exceptional ability to adapt. They are able to find support systems and maintain their cultural heritage while living in two worlds. They are making significant contributions to the Indian nation through a combination of roles that are often in conflict. They are pursuing careers in social work, law, and politics, yet they still teach their cultural heritage to their children and provide role models for their children and other women.

To a great extent, these women are experiencing role conflicts similar to women in the ambient society. They have, however, reduced their feelings of guilt and shame in the de-emphasis on homemaking by identifying the need for Indian leadership for both males and females in several areas. This is a response to oppressive external forces that threaten the survival of the American Indian reservation system and the preservation of cultural traditions.

The five women described are evidence of a growing self-awareness and self-assessment current among Indian women today. It is part of the larger issue of individual autonomy in a multicultural society. For these women, it means a different type of self-actualization and expression of potential than the restricted avenues of the past. In some instances their activity could be compared to that of a religious or political leader who is willing to sacrifice everything for a cause.

## Implications for the Future

The changing roles of Indian women are in direct response to the changes taking place within the local urban Indian community and on the national level. The decreasing number of eligible Indian men, increased educational opportunities, convenient day care facilities, concern for the health and welfare of Indian children, the elderly, and national energy policies are all forces that shape the status and role of Indian women. The urban environment, where other ethnic female role models, live is also a force that inspires Indian women to be more active in community affairs in contrast to their former passive role as women on the reservation. Indian women are becoming more active, but not necessarily to become liberated from Indian men. Their motivation is based on the survival of American Indians as a people. The goals of feminists are acknowledged to a lesser degree by urban Indian women. They instead see their husbands as having fewer job opportunities than themselves in a white-dominated society. Ethnic discrimination is a greater issue than sexual discrimination for Indian women. Indian women use their energy conservatively and, thus far, show little involvement in feminist movements.

Indian women are responding to external forces of oppression as well as internal forces crying for survival of a rich cultural tradition held holy and precious for thousands of years. Indian people are too small in number to restrict leadership to the male members. It is a time in history when Indian men and women must play many roles if they are to survive and keep their rich cultural heritage and their land base intact.

# References

Gridley, M. (1974). *Native American Women.* New York: Hawthorne.

Hallowell, I. (1967). "Ojibwa Personality and Acculturation." In Sol Tax, Acculturation in the Americas, (2nd ed.), (110). New York: Cooper Square.

Mead, M. (1932). *The Changing Culture of an Indian Tribe.* New York: Columbia University Press.

Medicine, B. (1977). *Role and Function of Indian Women in Indian Education.* Minneapolis: National Indian Education Association.

Medicine, B. (1978). *The Native American Woman: A Perspective.* Austin, TX.: National Educational Laboratory.

# Chapter 10

# Looking Back and Looking Forward

In reflecting on my childhood, adulthood, career, and now retirement, I have climbed many mountains and visited many valleys. They have all contributed to who I am today. I have no regrets because some of my darkest days helped me to know myself and my own strengths.

Today, modern life has alienated us from our ancient cultures, spiritual traditions, and ancient wisdom. Keeping balance with nature and balance within the body and the community contributes to the healing of ourselves.

Modern science has given us machines and technology to make life easier and an over abundance of information. People spend hours in superficial conversations on cell phones as if they are afraid to experience a moment of silence. These technologies and conveniences make life easier, but they do not necessarily lead to a healthier life or community.

It seems that we have fallen out of touch with our bodies' deeper rhythms and wisdom. We have become out of balance within ourselves. We can learn from the ancient cultures how to integrate mind and body and, thus, be more at peace within ourselves. The fast pace of a materialistic, consumer driven society is creating an unhealthy society, dependent on drugs for chronic illnesses and stress related disorders.

The millions of people who are addicted to illegal drugs and alcohol to alter their consciousness (and even today prescription drugs) are searching for spiritual experiences and connections. Spirituality is connectedness. We have become disconnected from humanity and the earth. We need to recover a sense of community and wholeness. Even though there is this pressing need to connect and achieve oneness with self and community, higher education continues to move further away and is not redressing this critical need. The churches have become political establishments, and many have lost all credibility for being centers for spiritual guidance.

It is unfortunate that higher education has become preoccupied with ego, pride, and money. The study of psychology has in many ways replaced religion for our society. Psychology is in need of change. Reductionism is being challenged. Reductionism created the lines of separation between the mind and the body, and it became superimposed over the spiritual domain as well. A paradigm was developed that separated God from Self. Anything of a spiritual nature has been considered subjective, irrational, and usually ignored. More emphasis has been placed on spirituality and the divine as being external, with less and less emphasis being placed on the internal.

We can learn much from indigenous cultures by examining their world view, their view of time, their relationships with family, and their spiritual practices. One need not embrace a specific religion, but can borrow those aspects of that religion that are meaningful to one's life. Each religion has something to offer. However, one need not be involved in any religion or organized group to find a spiritual experience or spiritual connection. One can find spirituality through art, music, dance, and even a walk through a park. Sitting among the trees and listening to the birds sing and watching the squirrels play can be a spiritual experience.

The wellness paradigm is ageless wisdom. It is based on the premise that the whole (mind, body, spirit, and emotion) is greater than the sum of its parts. Western science and academic knowledge are based on the Cartesian principle, or reductionist theory, through which truth (fact) is determined by separating and examining various pieces. Much spiritual phenomenon cannot be studied scientifically. Spirituality encompasses the total being and is superimposed on all of life's experiences. This is emphasized in the work of a number of authors/theorists, such as Joseph Campbell, Deepak Chopra, Larry Dossey, and the Dalai Lama, to name a few.

These authors present perspectives that honor the divine mystery. We can study consciousness, mythology, dream analysis, self actualization, prayer, and meditation to enhance our spiritual life. We an join discussion groups for spiritual guidance or organized churches if we so desire. We can take time to be silent and alone to reflect on our life's journey. Most of all, we can allocate time to find and follow our own spiritual path and discover that each of us is unique.

We may not be able to go on a vision quest but we can become aware of our unique gifts and talents which we are to share with humanity. We all have a purpose for living and/or a mission. It is up to each one of us to discover our purpose and to pursue goals that contribute to that purpose.

Spirituality can be found in music, and in my life, music has been very important. I spent 25 years singing in church choirs and community choral groups, and I taught myself to play the organ. In high school, I played the French horn and the baritone horn and participated in the marching band. Today, I spend many hours listening to CDs of my favorite musicians. Music lifts me to another level of consciousness of peace and comfort.

Western medicine has its value also. During the last ten years, I have had a hip replacement and new lenses replacing my original lenses which were clouded by cataracts. I believe that Western medicine has made great advances and is useful in many respects.

During my employment with the federal government, I traveled extensively. I took more than 600 flights in a period of four years. I have visited most of the states and most of our major cities. In addition, I have taken eight ocean cruises from Mexico to Vancouver, British Columbia and Alaska. I have traveled to Hawaii at least twelve times and spent time on each of the islands. I also traveled to Europe. There I visited France, Switzerland, and Italy. Travel has always been very enjoyable, and I am thankful that I spent time traveling when I was in excellent health. I have found people to be friendly and interesting to talk to in all of my travels. I believe people are basically good and want what is best for their families.

It is my hope that this brief account of my memoirs of raising a family and at the same time preparing myself to teach in universities may serve as an inspiration to other women to pursue their goals and fulfill their true potential in life.

# References

Campbell, J. (1968). *The Hero with A Thousand Faces.* Princeton, NJ: Princeton Bollinger.

Chopra, D. (1994). The *Seven Spiritual Laws of Success.* San Rafael, CA: New World Library.

Dalai Lama, H. H. (1999). *The Art of Happiness: A Handbook for Living.* New York: Riverhead Books.

Dossey, L. (1993). *Healing Words: The Power of Prayer and the Practice of Medicine.* San Francisco: Harper.

DuBray, W. (2001). *Spirituality and Healing: A Multicultural Perspective.* San Jose, CA: Writers Club Press.

# *Appendix A*

## Survey of American Indian Faculty

RECRUITMENT AND RETENTION
OF AMERICAN INDIAN FACULTY AND STAFF
CALIFORNIA STATE UNIVERSITY SYSTEM

A SURVEY


Submitted by

Dr. Wynne DuBray, Professor
    CSU Sacramento

and

Dr. Morgan Otis, Professor
    CSU Sacramento


July 7, 1994

CONTENTS

RECRUITMENT AND RETENTION
OF AMERICAN INDIAN FACULTY AND STAFF
CALIFORNIA STATE UNIVERSITY SYSTEM


INTRODUCTION

The American Indian Advisory Committee, Chancellors Office,
California State University System, established as a priority
a study to determine current issues and concerns of American
Indian faculty and staff within the system. The principal
investigators designated to conduct the study were Dr. Wynne
DuBray, Professor of Social Work and Dr. Morgan Otis, Professor
of Education at California State University Sacramento.

Statement of the Problem

The study was to identify the issues and concerns of American
Indian faculty and staff, in addition to the collection of
information on recruitment, assignments, retention, tenure and
departure from the California State University System.

Sources of Data

Two questionnaires developed by the investigators were mailed
to 151 faculty and staff members of the CSU system.  Forty
responses were received and formed the study sample.

Conclusions Reached

Analysis of the data reveals that most of the respondents are
male (25), are members of out of state tribes (31) and hold
Ph.Ds (19).  Most of the faculty respondents are tenured or
are in a tenure track (19) position.

As a group they have been productive in the development and
publication of 276 journal articles, 15 books and 29 chapters
in books.  Most of the respondents identify other ethnic groups
as faring better than they (29); however, they are for the most
part satisfied with their positions (22), and plan to stay with
the system until retirement.

The Problem

## Introduction

California is the home to 242,164 American Indians of more than
two hundred different tribal groups (1990 Census). It can be
assumed that due to the large American Indian population and
the ideal climate, California may also be the home of more
American Indians in higher education than any other state.

The California State University (CSU) System consists of 20
campuses throughout the state, employing more than 16,000 faculty
and serving more than 326,000 students. The CSU System offers
more than 1,500 bachelor's and master's degree programs in some
200 different subject areas. A limited number of doctoral
degrees are offered in collaboration with the University of
California and private institutions in California. Three of
the CSU campuses have been ranked by U.S. News & World Report
as among the top ten percent of regional colleges and
universities in the country.

Faculty salaries in the CSU system attract faculty from
throughout the country. The National Center for Education
Statistics (NCES) conducted a study of 3,025 institutions of
higher learning in 1991-92. This study states that average
faculty salaries in public institutions in California were found
to be the highest in the nation at $52,079 per year. The lowest
salaries in public institutions were found to be in Wyoming
at an annual rate of $29,961.

## Race and Ethnic Identity

The NCES national survey information from 1989 shows that 11
percent of college and university faculty are identified as
minority. The minority faculty represent the following
proportions by ethnic group: 3 percent are African American,
non-Hispanic, 2 percent Hispanic, 4 percent Asian or Pacific
Islander, and 1 percent American Indian/Alaska Native. Higher
education continues to lag in the hiring of minority faculty
(NEA, 1993).

California is more ethnically diverse than any other state in
the country and will become more diverse in the 1990s. Children
of color are a majority in California and make up over 87% of
students in the Los Angeles county school district. Whites
are a minority in San Francisco and Los Angeles.

Presently, there is a lack of knowledge pertaining to American
Indian faculty in California, specifically within the California

State University System. The goal of this project is to compile
and analyze data supplied by faculty and staff within the CSU
system. Some of the key concerns about faculty and staff to
be addressed are length of employment, level of education,
teaching and/or work assignments, tenure status, job
satisfaction, level of scholarly activity, tribal affiliation,
and access to mentors and faculty support systems.

## Statement of Collaboration

The researchers collaborated on all aspects of the project.
The development of the questionnaires was shared by both
researchers as were the logistics of the development of the
mailing list and the tasks of mailing the questionnaires.
Both researchers shared in the editing of the final draft.

## Background of the Problem

American Indians have had a long and painful relationship with
educational institutions. They have survived the boarding school
era of forced assimilation, sacrificing their language, culture,
religion and family support systems in the process of education.
Many American Indians have ambivalent feelings about Western
models of learning and find themselves alienated on university
campuses. Yet, American Indians are being seen graduating from
multiple disciplines with Ph.Ds and Masters degrees.

The percentage of American Indians who graduated from high school
increased from 51 percent in 1970 to 60 percent in 1980.
American Indian enrollments in colleges and universities across
the United States increased from 76,000 in 1976 to 90,000 in
1986 (Green and Tonnesen, 1991).

Our educational attainment improved during the 1980's. The
educational attainments levels of Americans Indians (including
Eskimos and Aleuts) improved significantly during the 1980's,
but remained considerably below the levels of the total
population. In 1990, 66 percent of the 1,080,000 American
Indians 25 years old and over were high school graduates or
higher compared with only 56 percent in 1980. Despite the
advances, the 1990 proportion was still below the total
population (75 percent).

American Indians were not as likely as the entire U.S. population
to have completed a bachelor's degree or higher. About 9 percent
of American Indians completed a bachelor's degree or higher
in 1990 compared with 8 percent in 1980-still lower than the
20 percent for the total population in 1990 (1990 Census).

## American Indians and Poverty

The proportion of American Indian (including Eskimo and Aleut)
persons and families living below the official Government poverty
level in 1989 was considerably higher than that of the total

population.  In 1989, about 603,000, or 31 percent, of American
Indians were living below the poverty level.  The national
poverty rate was about 13 percent (31.7 million persons).

Twenty-seven percent, or 125,000, American Indian families were
in poverty in 1989 compared with 10 percent of all families
(6.5 million).  Fifty percent of American Indian families
maintained by females with no husband present were in poverty
compared with 31 percent of all American families maintained
by women without husbands (1990, Census).

Half of the American Indians living on reservations live in
poverty.  A very high proportion, 51 percent, of the 437,431
American Indians residing on reservations and trust lands were
living below the poverty level in 1989.

There were vast differences in poverty rates in 1989 among the
10 largest reservations and trust lands.  About 2 in 3 persons
on the Papago, Pine Ridge, Gila River, and San Carlos
Reservations and trust lands were in poverty.  The Hopi,
Blackfeet, Zuni Pueblo, and Fort Apache Reservations had the
lowest percentages of American Indians in poverty, about 50
percent (1990 Census).


American Indian population on Reservations

The educational attainment rates differ substantially among
reservations.  The proportion of American Indian adults 25 years
old and over with high school diplomas or higher on the 10
largest reservations and trust lands ranged from 37 percent
to 66 percent.  Overall, 54 percent of American Indian adults
living on all reservations and trust lands were high school
graduates or higher.  Blackfeet and Hopi had similar proportions
(66 percent and 63 percent) of high school graduates or higher.
Rosebud and Pine Ridge Lakota had (59 percent and 55 percent)
of high school graduates or higher.  Gila River, at about 37
percent, had the lowest proportion of high school graduates
or higher, followed by Navajo with 41 percent.

When people are struggling to survive and provide their families
with the basic needs of food, shelter and clothing, higher
education is only a dream.  The attainment of a masters degree
or a doctorate for most American Indians is a major
accomplishment just in terms of financing one's education.
Add to the financial struggles, the many cultural conflicts
American Indians face in every aspect of living and one becomes
aware of the tremendous challenges American Indian students,
staff and faculty face on a daily basis.

American Indians have a rich cultural heritage in common as
well as tribal uniqueness to be shared  in institutions of
learning.  As the people indigenous to North America, they have
a greater sense of history than most Americans and possess a

value system of cooperation rather than competition that dates back thousands of years. They have much to teach to the masses.

Statement of the Research Problem

The research problem is the lack of data about American Indian faculty and staff within the California State University System.

Purpose of the Study

The primary purpose is to gather information from American Indian faculty and staff within the California State University System in order to evaluate how well they are doing professionally, and how they perceive their role in public higher education. This information will be used by the American Indian Advisory Committee and the Chancellors office to make improvements in program planning and professional development opportunities for advancement for American Indians within the CSU system.

Theoretical Framework

A general systems theory approach is best utilized in the evaluation of the response of large educational institutions to minority populations such as American Indian faculty and staff. Greene and Ephross (1991) describe a social system as a defined structure of interdependent and interacting individuals that have the capacity for organized activity. Longres (1990) sees systems as groups of individuals, sharing a common identity and assigned roles and statuses, and divided into departments and units. This best describes the CSU system within which the American Indian faculty and staff are active participants.

## Methodology
Design

An evaluation research design was selected as the method best suited for this study of the status of American Indian Faculty and Staff within the California State University System. The purpose of evaluation research is to assess and improve the planning, administration, implementation, effectiveness efficiency, and utility of educational institutions and the services they deliver.

Some common examples of information gathered through evaluative research is to obtain a sampling of subject responses to questions pertinent to the participation of specific minority populations within a large bureaucratic institution of higher learning. In addition, information can be collected which can be used to improve program planning and expedite problem solution when conflicts arise within institutions.

Subjects

The population being studied is the American Indian faculty
and staff employed in the twenty universities that make up the
California State University System.

It was hoped that all of the 151 questionnaires would be
returned. Fifteen questionnaire packets were returned due to
the subject either being deceased or no longer with the
institution. Forty questionnaires were returned. The 40
respondents constitute a non-random sample of the total
population of faculty and staff within the CSU system.
Participation in the study was voluntary. In order to protect
confidentiality and anonymity no follow-up requests were made
for the return of the questionnaires. It was important to
respect and protect the right to confidentiality and anonymity.

The results of this study may not be representative of the
population being studied. Therefore, no generalizations can
be made from these responses to the general population of CSU
faculty and staff, since the response rate was only 30 percent.
However, the information collected is of value from a case study
perspective. The information can be used to gain a profile
of faculty and staff and their opinions and concerns as they
work within the CSU system.

Instrumentation

Two questionnaires were developed, one for staff and one for
faculty. Faculty and staff have different advancement paths
and different roles within the university and therefore special
instruments were needed.

The questionnaire (Appendix A) for the staff consisted of 24
questions covering demographic information, level of education,
work environment, support systems, recruitment and job
satisfaction.

The questionnaire (Appendix A) for the faculty consisted of
50 questions covering demogrphic information, work environment,
tenure status, teaching assignments, level of education, support
systems, recruitment and job satisfaction.

The questionnaires were mailed to the university addresses of
personnel identifying themselves as American Indian on personnel
records. A prepaid and self-addressed envelope was provided
as further incentive to return the questionnaire.

The questionnaires were designed in a manner that allowed the
respondent to circle most answers and would not require a great
amount of time in filling them out.

Data Gathering Procedures

This study was conducted with the support of the CSU Chancellors office in Long Beach, California. The list of American Indian faculty and staff was provided by the staff of the Chancellors office.

A cover letter explaining the purpose of the study and requesting a response was sent to each subject along with the consent form (Appendix A) and a stamped, self-addressed envelope. Fourteen of the questionnaire packets were returned due to subjects no longer being employed by that university.

The data was compiled and analyzed and organized into an easily understandable and useful format for review.

Protection of Human Subjects

The instruments used in the study were developed and designed by the researchers and submitted to the university committee for the protection of human subjects . Approval was granted. None of the questions posed a risk to the subjects. The only risk would be possible harm from exposure to loss of anonymity. Since participation in the study was entirely voluntary, and consent forms were separated from anonymous questionnaires immediately upon receipt of questionnaires the identity of respondents is fully protected. Furthermore the data is reported in aggregate form to provide increased protection and anonymity.


Analysis of Data

Forty completed questionnaires were received and analyzed. Of these 40 responses, 25 were male and 15 were female. The highest frequency of tribal affiliation was Cherokee, numbering 7. A total of 21 tribes were represented with 5 tribes native to California. The number of years working in the CSU System ranged from 1 to 26 years. Twenty-five faculty and fifteen staff returned the questionnaires.

The 40 respondents consisted of both faculty and staff (mostly counselors). Of these 2 held AA degrees, 4 held BA degrees, 15 held masters degrees and 19 held Ph.D's.

Table 1.

| Questions 6. (N=14) | Department's committment to hiring American Indians | | | |
|---|---|---|---|---|
| | Very serious | Serious | Not serious | Don't Know |
| Responses | 4 | 2 | 6 | 2 |

Question 7.  University administration's committment to hiring American Indians.

Responses:
8 No
2 Yes

Question 8.  Does a particular group fare better than other minority groups in the department?

Responses:
2  No
11 Yes

Question 9.  Groups faring better than American Indians:

Responses:
7 named African Americans
7 named Hispanics
3 named Asian Americans
2 named Anglo Americans

Question 10. Conduciveness of the working environment for all staff:

Responses:
6 responded  Always conducive
6 responded  Sometimes conducive
1 responded  Seldom conducive
1 responded  Never conducive

Question 11. Conduciveness of the work environment for American Indian staff:

Responses:
6 responded Always conducive
5 responded Sometimes conducive
2 responded Seldom conducive
1 responded Never conducive

Question 12. Supportiveness of the administration in helping
American Indian staff achieve objectives:

Responses:
6 Responded Always supportive
4 Responded Sometimes supportive
3 Responded Seldom supportive
1 Responded Never supportive

Question 13.  Opportunity for American Indian staff to
participate in decision-making that affects the program:

Responses:
6 Responded High
2 Responded Medium
4 Responded Low
2 Responded None

Question 14. Level of institutional racism in office:

Responses:
0 Responded  High
3 Responded  Medium
8 Responded  Low
3 Responded  None

Question 15.  Level of harassment of American Indian staff
by Administration:

Responses:
1 Responded  High
4 Responded  Medium
1 Responded  Low
8 Responded  None

Question 16.  Minority status in this program environment is:

Responses:
2 Responded  At risk
1 Responded  A disadvantage
4 Responded  Neither advantage or disadvantage
3 Responded  An advantage
4 Responded  A definite asset

Question 17. Years employed in the system:

Responses:  Ranged from 1 to 25 years.

Question 18. Have filed a grievance in order to be retained
or promoted:

Responses:  13 No
0 Yes

Question 19. What special needs and concerns do you have as
            a staff person?

Lack of support for the retention of American Indian students.
No committment to hire American Indian faculty.
Too much micro-management of administration.
Job classification doesn't fit the duties.
No job security like tenure for faculty.
Too many threats of cutbacks.
Would like to see professional staff treated with more respect.
Would like to work flex time in order to attend.
ceremonies,funerals and community meetings.
There is no committment to recruit American Indian staff, faculty
or students.
Not enough effort to recruit American Indian students.
I am over extended trying to work for both the university and
in the community.
We need more support services for American Indian students and
a more committed student recruitment program.

Question 20.  Do you have access to an American Indian support
group?
Responses: 8 Yes
           5 No

Question 21.  What Cultural concessions have been required of
you as an American Indian staff person within CSU?

Responses:

Our ceremonies are not respected as holy days are for other
groups.
We are shown off for visitors as token Indians.
Having to use my vacation for ceremonies, since our holy days
do not fall on Christian holidays.
I am always having to explain my responsibility to my community
and receive very little understanding from my co-workers.

Question 22.  Plans to stay or leave the CSU System

Responses:   7  Staying
             4  Leaving
             3  Do not know

Question 23.  How were you recruited for your position?

Responses:
5  Recruited by a Friend
7  Responded to a job announcement

Question 24.  Would you recommend CSU employment to your friends?

Responses:  12  Yes
             1  No

FACULTY RESPONSES

Of the 25 faculty responses, 8 were lecturers, 2 were Assistant
Professors, 2 were Associate Professors and 13 were Full
Professors. Fifteen faculty taught at both the BA and Masters
level. They taught in a variety of disciplines. They published
a total of 276 journal articles, 15 books and 29 chapters in
books. They held a total of 37 leadership positions.

Most of the faculty, 54%, did not feel that either
the department or the university in which they worked held a
serious commitment in hiring of American Indian faculty.


Most of the faculty, 58%, did not feel their department or
university has been successful in hiring American Indian faculty.

Most of the faculty, 75%, felt that other ethnic groups fare
better then they, with 62%, naming Euro-Americans as getting
favored treatment over all minorities. African Americans were
considered by 30% as getting more favored treatment than American
Indians, with 20% naming Hispanics as getting more favored
treatment than American Indians and only 4% percent naming Asians
as getting favored treatment over American Indians.

Less than half saw the overall environment as being conducive
to a pleasant work situation for American Indian faculty. Less
than half, 44% of the American Indian faculty felt their
Chair/Director was supportive of them in achieving their
professional goals. Less than half of the American Indian
faculty, 40%, felt that the opportunity to participate in
decision-making was either high or very high. Some 20% of the
American Indian faculty felt that the opportunity to participate
in decision-making was either low to very low to none.

Opportunities for leadership roles for American Indian faculty
in their department was seen as high or very high by 44%.
Some 30% of American Indian faculty saw opportunities for
leadership as low to very low to none.

Level of institutional racism in their department/programs was
seen by American Indian faculty as low to very low by 37% with
12% seeing it as high to very high.

Level of harassment of American Indian faculty by administration
was seen as low to very low to none, by 62%.

Demands on the time of American Indian faculty members to serve
on committees because of their race/ethnicity was seen as high

or very high by 37%. Demands on the time of American Indian faculty to give lectures/presentations on campus related to ethnicity was seen as low to very low by 44%.

On the subject of whether their department practices the principles of equal employment opportunity, 62% of the American Indian faculty reported in the affirmative. Some 54% of American Indian faculty see their minority status as neither an advantage nor a disadvantage.

In regard to remaining employed in the CSU system, 62% of those responding plan to remain employed in the system. This is also the same percentage of respondents who reported as being tenured. One third, 33% of the faculty had filed grievances in order to be retained, tenured or promoted. Several respondents communicated with one of the researchers by telephone, requested to remain anonymous and were afraid to respond in writing. These subjects were working in very hostile environments and would not identify their campus location.

In the area of recruitment, 40% responded to an announcement of the position, 37% were told about the position by a friend and encouraged to apply.

Some 44% of the American Indian faculty serve on a university senate or campus-wide committee. Most, 58%, do not have access to a mentor and 46% do not have access to an American Indian support group.

## CONCLUSIONS & IMPLICATIONS

Conclusions

This study was designed to evaluate and identify the needs and concerns of American Indian faculty and staff, in addition to the collection of information on recruitment, assignments, retention, tenure and departure from the California State University System.

Faculty and staff were asked to complete a questionnaire about their present status within the CSU system. Separate questionnaires were sent to faculty and staff.

Both faculty and staff did not see the CSU system as serious about recruitment of American Indian students, faculty or staff. Both faculty and staff saw other groups faring better than they in recruitment and retention of students, faculty and staff. Staff saw Hispanics and African Americans faring better, while faculty saw Euro-Americans faring better than all minorities. One third of the faculty had filed grievances in order to become tenured or promoted.

The CSU system is seen as a conducive working environment by
less than half of the American Indian staff and faculty.
A list of eleven (11) concerns were voiced by staff and faculty.
These concerns reflect alienation, lack of mentors, lack of
support systems on campus (45%) percent, lack of sensitivity
regarding their  culture by colleagues, and cultural value
conflict in many areas.

Cultural concessions fell into 4 categories, spirituality,
tokenism, insensitivity to community responsibility and lack
of respect for cultural ceremonies by the system.

The majority of faculty see their minority status as neither
an advantage or a disadvantage.  Very few faculty or staff were
actively recruited by the university, most heard about positions
through friends or job announcements.

The faculty respondents were active in scholarly activities,
publishing 276 journal articles, 15 books and 29 chapters in
books.

Implications

The CSU system should examine its recruitment and retention
practices for American Indian students, staff and faculty.
While the system is doing well in some areas, there are other
areas that need improvement.  It appears that there is very
little active recruitment of this population within the system.

American Indian faculty are discouraged from researching or
writing about their own ethnic group and are penalized, while
Euro-Americans are rewarded for research on their ethnic groups.
This is clearly a double standard which penalizes American
Indians and creates unfair criteria for tenure and promotion.
American Indian journals are not recognized as refereed journals
by many tenure committees which clearly discriminates against
American Indian faculty who choose to write about their ethnic
population.

Sensitivity training for non-Indian faculty and staff on American
Indian Cultures is needed to create greater understanding about
community obligations and American Indian spirituality and
philosophy.

The survival of American Indian faculty is at risk.  There is
a great need for mentoring within the CSU system.  American
Indian faculty without mentors express frustration and worry
that they may not be focusing their energy on the right goals
for career development and advancement.

Working through the tenure and promotion maze requires support
from senior faculty mentors.  Some 78% percent of minority
faculty feel they face widespread barriers in this process.
When scholarship is based upon publication in Euro-American

dominated journals, the American Indian faculty is usually at a great disadvantage.

American Indian faculty are successful in bringing in funds through grantwriting but usually are overburdened with the responsibility of managing these programs. They remain on soft money positions while their counterparts move into tenure track positions. Grantwriting in many universities is not considered "scholarly" activity and does not carry much weight in the tenure process.

A major concern is the high rate of faculty (33%) who must resort to the grievance process in order to become retained, tenured or promoted. An internal investigation should be conducted to compare tenure and promotion rates of American Indian faculty with other ethnic groups including Euro-Americans to determine if they (American Indians) are being treated fairly in the process.

This study has been an initial attempt to evaluate the status of American Indian faculty and staff within the CSU system. It is suggested that an attempt be made to increase the size of the sample from approximately a third to at least half of the populaltion of interest. Although 40 faculty and staff responded, approximately 97 did not. Of the 97 who did not respond, one could raise the question as to the number of faculty who identify as American Indians but who cannot provide proof of membership in any tribal group. Recently the issue of ethnic fraud in higher education has come to light through media coverage. The number of American Indians in higher education may be totally inaccurate due to this fraud. Perhaps the CSU system should require that applicants to their institutions who claim to be American Indian prove that they are.

It is not known how representative the 40 respondents were of the total pool of subjects. Future surveys might offer incentives to encourage more subjects to respond.

# BIBLIOGRAPHY

Catalog, California State University, Sacramento, 1994-95.

DuBray, Wynne (1992). HUMAN SERVICES AND AMERICAN INDIANS, West Publishing, St. Paul.

Green, D. E. & Tonnesen, T. V., (1991). AMERICAN INDIAN: SOCIAL JUSTICE AND PUBLIC POLICY, University of Wisconsin, Milwaukee, Wi.

Greene, R. R. , & Ephross, P. H. (1991). HUMAN BEHAVIOR THEORY AND SOCIAL WORK PRACTICE. New York: Aldine De Gruyer.

Longres, J. F. (1990). HUMAN BEHAVIOR IN THE SOCIAL ENVIRONMENT. Illinois: F. E. Peacock Publishers.

The NEA 1993 Almanac of Higher Education, (1993),Washington, D.C.

The United States Department of Commerce, U. S. Census Report, 1990.

THOUGHT AND ACTION, NEA Higher Education Journal, Spring 1994, Volume X, Number 1.

# Cover Letter and Questionnaires

# QUESTIONNAIRE FOR AMERICAN INDIAN FACULTY
## IN THE CALIFORNIA STATE UNIVERSITIES

1. Years of service at CSU ___          2. Gender  M__  F__

3. Tribe and/or Nation _____

4. Education:

| | Type of degree | Major or concentration | Year degree awarded | University where degree received |
|---|---|---|---|---|
| Undergraduate | | | | |
| Graduate | | | | |
| Doctorate | | | | |

5. Indicate your faculty rank(s) over the life of your career in a university setting. Place a zero in the box if you have never been at that particular rank.

### Faculty Rank

| | Lecturer | Assistant Professor | Associate Professor | Full Professor | Adjunct Professor | Other (specify) |
|---|---|---|---|---|---|---|
| Number of Years at this Rank | | | | | | |

How many years did it take you to be advanced to your present faculty rank? _____

6. Tenure status: Check appropriate column.

Tenured ____   Tenure track ____   Non-tenure track ____

If tenured, how long have you been tenured? _____

If tenure track, what year will tenure decision be made? _____

12. How many elected and/or appointed leadership positions do you hold in American Indian organizations?

Specify # ___   Title(s) _____


## PART B

The next part of the questionnaire pertains to the Department or Program where you presently are employed.


13. Department-Faculty composition:

a. Total number of faculty employed at your Department ___

b. Number of minority faculty employed ___
   (For the purpose of this study, count only those individuals who are African-American, American Indian, Asian American, Hispanic, or Puerto Rican as minority faculty.)

c. How many are:

African-American ___      Hispanic ___
American Indian ___       Puerto Rican ___
Asian-American ___        Other ___ (specify) _____


14. What is the racial background of your Chair/Director?

African-American ___      Hispanic ___
American Indian ___       Puerto Rican ___
Anglo-American ___        Asian-American ___
Other ___(specify) _____


15. What is the racial background of your school dean?

African-American ___      Hispanic ___
American Indian ___       Puerto Rican ___
Anglo-American ___        Asian-American ___
Other ___ (specify) _____


16. Type of programs your department offers:

Doctorate & Master's degree ___    Master's & Undergraduate ___
Master's degree only ___           Undergraduate only ___

22. Conduciveness of the overall working environment of your Department for <u>all faculty</u>:

    1 Always Conducive    2 Usually Conducive    3 Sometimes Conducive    4 Seldom Conducive

    5 Never Conducive    0 Don't Know/No Opinion

23. Conduciveness of the overall working environment of your Department for American Indian Faculty:

    1 Always Conducive    2 Usually Conducive    3 Sometimes Conducive    4 Seldom Conducive

    5 Never Conducive    0 Don't Know/No Opinion

24. Supportiveness of the Chair/Director in helping <u>all faculty members</u> achieve their professional goals.

    1 Always Supportive    2 Usually Supportive    3 Sometimes Supportive    4 Seldom Supportive

    5 Never Supportive    0 Don't Know/No Opinion

25. Supportiveness of the Chair/Director in helping American Indian faculty achieve their professional goals.

    1 Always Supportive    2 Usually Supportive    3 Sometimes Supportive    4 Seldom Supportive

    5 Never Supportive    0 Don't Know/No Opinion

26. Supportiveness of <u>faculty (as a group)</u> in helping <u>all faculty members</u> achieve their professional goals.

    1 Always Supportive    2 Usually Supportive    3 Sometimes Supportive    4 Seldom Supportive

    5 Never Supportive    0 Don't Know/No Opinion

27. Supportiveness of faculty (as a group) in helping American Indian faculty achieve their professional goals.

    1 Always Supportive    2 Usually Supportive    3 Sometimes Supportive    4 Seldom Supportive

    5 Never Supportive    0 Don't Know/No Opinion

28. Opportunity for <u>all faculty</u> to participate in decision-making that affects your department/program.

    1 Very high    2 High    3 Medium or average    4 Low

    5 Very low to none    0 Don't Know/No Opinion

36. Demand on the time of <u>all faculty members</u> to serve on committees.

    1 Very high    2 High    3 Medium to average    4 Low

    5 Very low to none    0 Don't Know/No Opinion

37. Demand on your time to serve on committees because of your race/ethnicity.

    1 Very high    2 High    3 Medium to average    4 Low

    5 Very low to none    0 Don't Know/No Opinion

38. Demand on your time to give lectures/presentations to classes and groups on campus on topics related to your race/culture.

    1 Very high    2 High    3 Medium to average    4 Low

    5 Very low to none    0 Don't Know/No Opinion

39. Demand on your time to give lectures/presentations to community groups on topics related to your race/culture.

    1 Very high    2 High    3 Medium or average    4 Low

    5 Very low to none    0 Don't Know/No Opinion

40. Does your department practice the principles of equal employment opportunity?

    1 Very frequently    2 Frequently    3 Occasionally    4 Seldom

    5 Not at all    0 Don't Know/No Opinion

41. In this department environment my minority status is (circle one number):

    5 At Risk    4 A Disadvantage    3 Neither an Advantage nor Disadvantage

    2 An Advantage    1 A Definite Asset

42. Please indicate your plans relative to staying or leaving your present position. Also, give a <u>brief</u> rationale for staying or leaving your present position.

49. What are your special needs and concerns as a faculty person in the CSU system? List below:

50. As an American Indian, what cultural concessions have been required of you as a faculty person in the CSU system? (Explain)

11. Conduciveness of the overall working environment of your program for American Indian staff.

| 1 | 2 | 3 | 4 |
|---|---|---|---|
| always conducive | sometimes conducive | seldom conducive | never conducive |

12. Supportiveness of the administration in helping American Indian staff achieve objectives.

| 1 | 2 | 3 | 4 |
|---|---|---|---|
| always supportive | sometimes supportive | seldom supportive | never supportive |

13. Opportunity for American Indian staff to participate in decision-making that affects your program.

| 1 | 2 | 3 | 4 |
|---|---|---|---|
| High | Medium | Low | None |

14. Level of institutional racism in your office.

| 1 | 2 | 3 | 4 |
|---|---|---|---|
| High | Medium | Low | None |

15. Level of harassment of American Indian staff in your program by administration.

| 1 | 2 | 3 | 4 |
|---|---|---|---|
| High | Medium | Low | None |

16. In this program environment my minority status (circle one number):

1. At risk
2. A disadvantage
3. Neither an advantage or disadvantage
4. An advantage
5. A definite asset

17. How many years have you been employed in the CSU system? ____

18. Have you ever filed a grievance in order to be retained or promoted? ____ If yes, please explain: _____

_____
_____
_____
_____
_____

# QUESTIONNAIRE FOR AMERICAN INDIAN STAFF IN THE CALIFORNIA STATE UNIVERSITIES

## Part A

1. Gender: M_____ F_____

2. Tribe and/or Nation: _____

3. Education: High school ____ BA ____ MA ____

4. Job Title: _____

5. Location of your University: _____
   _____

6. Is there a serious commitment on the part of the department's administration to hire American Indians?

   | 1 | 2 | 3 | 4 |
   |---|---|---|---|
   | very serious | serious | not serious | don't know |

7. Is there a serious commitment on the part of the University administration to hire American Indians?

8. Does a particular group(s) fare better than other minority groups(s) in your department?

   Yes _____     No ____

9. If you answered yes in question 8, please check all applicable groups(s) you believe fare(s) better than American Indians.

   African-American ____     Hispanic ____     Asians ____

   Anglo-American ____     Other ____ (specify): _____

## Part B

The following questions are to elicit information on the general working conditions in your program for American Indian staff.

10. Conduciveness of the overall working environment of your program for all staff.

    | 1 | 2 | 3 | 4 |
    |---|---|---|---|
    | Always conducive | sometimes conducive | seldom conducive | never conducive |

19. What special needs and concerns do you have as a staff person? _____

    _____
    _____
    _____

20. Do you have access to an American Indian support group? ____

    _____

21. As an American Indian, what cultural concessions have been required of you as a staff person in the CSU system? (explain):

    _____
    _____
    _____

22. Please indicate your plans relative to staying or leaving your present position. Also, give a brief rationale for staying or leaving your present position: _____

    _____
    _____
    _____

23. How were you recruited for this position? (explain):

    _____
    _____
    _____

24. Would you recommend your American Indian friends to seek employment with the CSU system? Yes ____ No ____

    Please give reasons for your answer to No. 24. _____

    _____
    _____

*****************************************************************

# *Appendix B*

## Lecture Guide Manual on Spirituality Course

# SW 232 Spirituality & Social Work

## CSUSacramento

## Dr. Wynne DuBray

## Lecture Guide Manual

Is there a spiritual site you have alw ays wanted to visit?

A Ceremony you are curious about?

Open your mind and heart to the experience.


1. Set an intention and write it down,
2. Where are you going and Why
3. Write a 2 page response to include:  Your experience of what you saw, felt, heard and smelled.

# CLASS PRESENTATIONS TOPICS

Spiritual healing and vodun voodoo

Grace

The Power of Music

Spiritual Journey through Song

Prayer

Out of Body Experiences

Integrating Spirituality into Health Care at End of Life

Spirituality of Narcotics Anonymous/Alcoholics Anonymous

Labyrinth and Its Uses

Spirituality/Healing / Animals/Pets

Curanderismo

Communicating with the Spirits

Childrens' Grief

Spirituality and Music

Near Death Experiences

Meditation

Spirituality and loss/grief

PTSD & Spirituality

Chakras

Spiritual Healing & Color

Healing and Psychobody work

## Reiki

# THE THREE Cs OF SPIRITUALITY

## CONNECTION

Moving from beyond your little , isolated ego or personality into connection with something bigger, within or outside yourself.

## COMPASSION

Softening towards yourself or others by "feeling with" rather than being against yourself, others of the world.

## CONTRIBUTION

Being of unselfish service to others or the world.

# SEVEN PATHWAYS TO SPIRITUALITY
# THROUGH CONNECTION

---

1. Connection to the soul, the deeper self, the spirit

2. Connection to through the body

3. Connection to another

4. Connection to community

5. Connection through nature

6. Connection by participating in making or appreciating art

7. Connection to the Universe or higher power or God or Cosmic consciousness

# ELEMENTS OF RELIGIONS THAT CAN BE INCORPORATED INTO SPIRITUALITY

1.  RITUAL

2.  GROUP ACTION AND INTERACTION, FINDING OR DEVELOPING LIKE-MINDED PEOPLE, DOING SOCIAL ACTION OR GOOD WORKS IN GROUPS.

3.  CONNECTING TO SOMETHING BIGGER THAN SELF

4.  FINDING ATONEMENT AFTER IMMORAL OR SHAMEFUL ACTS, THOUGHTS OR FEELINGS

5.  DEVELOPING A MORAL SENSIBILITY

# SOLUTION-ORIENTED SPIRITUALITY

## 1. REVISITING A SPIRITUAL MOMENT OR TIME

## 2. RECREATE THE EXPERIENCE

## 3. BRING THAT SENSE OF SPIRITUALITY TO ANY SITUATION IN WHICH YOU ARE HAVING CURRENT DIFFICULTY OR ANTICIPATE HAVING DIFFICULTY IN THE FUTURE

# ASSUMPTIONS OF A SPIRITUAL APPROACH TO THERAPY

1. PEOPLE ARE NOT DEFINED BY OR DETERMINED BY THE CIRCUMSTANCES OF THEIR LIVES. THERE IS MORE TO PEOPLE THAN NATURE OR NURTURE, PERSONALITY, GENETICS, BIOCHEMISTRY OR CAUSE AND EFFECT.

2. PEOPLE HAVE SPIRITUAL RESOURCES, EVEN WHEN THEY ARE NOT RELIGIOUS OR WHEN THEY PROFESS NO SPIRITUAL SENSIBILITIES OR BELIEFS.

3. THERAPISTS CAN BRING A SPIRITUAL SENSIBILITY INTO THERAPY WITHOUT IMPOSING IT ON CLIENTS.

4. PEOPLE HAVE ALREADY DEVELOPED WAYS OF TAPPING INTO A SENSE OF SOMETHING BIGGER THAN THEMSELVES.

5. DRAWING ON SPIRITUAL RESOURCES CAN FACILITATE THERAPY OUTCOMES.

6. RELIGION IS DISTINCT FROM SPIRITUALITY FOR SOME PEOPLE.

# SPIRITUALITY IN THERAPY ASSESSMENT

# 1. SPIRITUAL HISTORY

# 2. SPIRITUAL RESOURCES AND SOLUTIONS

# 3. SPIRITUAL HOPES AND INTENTIONS

## ASSESSMENT OF SPIRITUALITY

**Identify stress buffers: sources of meaning**

**Identify religious/spiritual coping methods**
       **Associated with better or poorer**
        **Mental/physical adjustment to stress**
        **i.e. prayer**

**May include:**
**Clinicians' potential biases**

**Clarification of values**

**DSM IV's Diagnosis of Religious or Spiritual Problem: V62.89**

**Loss or questioning of faith**
**Problems associated with conversion to a new faith,**
**Questioning of Spiritual Values that may be related to an organized church or religious institution**
**Questions arising from near-death or mystical experiences**

# SPIRITUAL INTERVENTIONS:

Pursue middle ground in attempting to modify destructive religious beliefs, such as those leading clients to:
Avoid reality and responsibility
Behave self=destructively (stay with an abusive partner)
Have false expectations of God(promise of a problem free life)

# CRISES COUNSELING

Heart Attack, Cancer, Spinal cord injury, Impaired Fertility, Stroke, Chronic illnesses
Can be viewed as either a danger or an opportunity – dependent on meaning the client makes of the event.

# SPIRITUALLY RELATED SOURCES OF MEANING:

Deeper connection with & compassion for others
Facing mortality & greater acceptance of death
Increased commitment to one's spiritual self

# 12 STEP PROGRAMS:

Addiction & spirituality

# Appendix C

## Pictures

*Back row:* **Emma Anderson and Myrtle Kewley (older sisters)
Wynne DuBray is in the front row.**

Violet Rocek is on the left, Wynne DuBray is on the right

Wynne DuBray

**Wynne DuBray and (soul mate) Joseph Lipoma**

*Back Row:* Ken DuBray, Alvina Van Epps, Wynne, Emma Anderson, Leona Pechota. *Front Row:* Myrtle Kewley and Violet Rocek Not Shown

is Delbert DuBray, these are my sibling

My sons, David Hanson, Wynne, Les Hanson

Yvonne Hanson, My deceased daughter

My deceased parents, Lilian and Peter DuBray

My deceased maternal grandmother, Louise High Bear Rice

Wynne DuBray

**Wynne DuBray**

Wynne, Ken, Les, Back Row, Yvonne & David

**Delbert DuBray**